VISIBLE WORDS

THE SANDARS LECTURES FOR 1964

JOHN SPARROW

VISIBLE WORDS

A STUDY OF

INSCRIPTIONS

IN AND AS

BOOKS AND WORKS OF ART

O seule et sage voix
Qui chantes pour les yeux!

VALÉRY

CAMBRIDGE
AT THE UNIVERSITY PRESS
1969

Published by the Syndics of the Cambridge University Press
Bentley House, 200 Euston Road, London N.W.1
American Branch: 32 East 57th Street, New York, N.Y.10022

© Cambridge University Press 1969

Library of Congress Catalogue Card Number: 68-10027

Standard Book Number: 521 06534 8

Printed in Great Britain
at the University Printing House, Cambridge
(Brooke Crutchley, University Printer)

Illustrations printed by D. H. Greaves, Limited, Scarborough

To
Kenneth Clark

CONTENTS

ACKNOWLEDGEMENTS

The author and publishers are grateful for permission
to reproduce the following photographs:

3, 4(*a*), 4(*b*) from Kirchner/Klaffenbach, *Imagines Inscriptionum Atticarum*, Gebr. Mann Verlag, Berlin; 5 from Diehl, *Inscriptiones Latinae Christianae Veteres*, Weidmann, Berlin; 6 Mansell–Anderson; 7, 8 Mansell–Alinari; 9 Publifoto; 17, 18, 19 Mansell–Anderson; 20 Mansell–Alinari; 21 National Gallery of Art, Washington, D.C., Samuel H. Kress Collection; 22 Mansell–Anderson; 23 Bulloz, Paris; 24, 25 Mansell–Alinari; 26, 27, 28 Mansell–Anderson; 29 Mansell–Brogi; 30 The National Gallery, London; 31 Gallerie del'Accademia, Venice; 32 The Trustees of the Chatsworth Settlement; 33 Mansell–Giraudon; 34 Miss Katherine E. McBride, President, Bryn Mawr College, and Miss Caroline Newton; 35 Ashmolean Museum, Oxford; 36 from Hartt, Corti and Kennedy, *The Chapel of the Cardinal of Portugal*, University of Pennsylvania Press; 36 detail, Fototeca Berenson, The Harvard University Center for Italian Renaissance Studies, Villa I Tatti, Florence; 37 *Denkmäler der Renaissance-Sculptur in Italien*, F. Bruckmann A.-G., Munich, 1899; 38 Mansell–Alinari; 39, 40 Mansell–Anderson; 41 Mansell–Alinari; 42 Mansell–Brogi; 43 Vatican Museum; 44 Mansell–Brogi; 45 Mansell–Anderson.

ILLUSTRATIONS

CHAPTER III

CHAPTER IV

All the illustrations have been reduced in reproduction, except for Plates 49 and 50, which have been enlarged.

PREFACE

This volume contains the four lectures—with their text expanded and altered so as to make them more nearly fit for publication—that I delivered, under the title *The Inscription and the Book*, as Sandars Lecturer in Bibliography at Cambridge in 1964.

The electors must, I fancy, have found themselves in difficulties in their search for a Sandars Lecturer before they decided to approach someone whose claims to be called a bibliographer were as tenuous as mine; and I was punished for the vanity that induced me to accept the honour by the difficulty that I for my part experienced in finding a subject in the field of bibliography on which I was qualified to speak. However, the interest I had taken over many years in the history since the Renaissance of the inscription, both as a form of art and as the subject or the matter of published books, had led me to become acquainted with the works of Emanuele Tesauro and his followers, and the effusion of 'lapidary' books by these composers all over Europe in the seventeenth century seemed to be an episode in the history of literature and of book-production interesting and unfamiliar enough to provide a topic suitable for the occasion. My third lecture, which deals with the genesis and history of the lapidary book—though no doubt it will be superseded (if anyone thinks the subject worthy of further attention) by studies displaying wider knowledge and deeper *expertise*—is at least, I believe, an original excursion in a field that may, by a slight stretching of the term, be called bibliographical.

My first lecture also may suggest to professed bibliographers a line worth pursuing: there is room for a comprehensive guide to publications in the field of post-classical epigraphy, including not only collections of the works of individual composers but also repertories of inscriptions belonging to particular countries, districts, or towns (like those of Schrader, Forcella, Cicogna, Galletti, de Guilherminy, Weever, and le Neve) and collections and anthologies (like Aicher's, Fendt's and Popham's) drawn from a wider variety of sources.

The claim of the two remaining lectures to be called bibliographical is even slighter. In the fourth, which served as a sort of *bonne bouche* to close the series, I touched lightly upon some of the aesthetic questions that present themselves to anyone who considers the inscription as a form of literature; my aim in the second was to remind my audience of the prominence and frequency of the inscription as a 'property' on the stage of Renaissance life.

The part played by inscriptions in architecture and painting has not, I suspect, been appreciated to the full by art critics and historians, and the subject fascinated me so strongly that I found myself, as I revised my second lecture, forgetting bibliography and adding more and more illustrative examples, so that the text I eventually presented to the printer was disproportionately long compared with its fellows, and bore but a faint resemblance to the discourse that I actually delivered.

In thus plunging into the sea of art-historical criticism, I know well that I am invading waters inhabited by carnivores who may be glad, as they see him floundering in the depths, to make short work of an intruder. I can only hope that expert critics will bear in mind that my suggestions—such as those concerning Palladio's façade of S. Francesco della Vigna (pp. 41–8), Botticelli's *Madonna of the Magnificat* (pp. 53–7), and Moretto's *Salome* (pp. 76–9)—are put forward tentatively, and in the hope that they may stimulate further inquiries on their part, and I trust that they will judge my theories the less and not the more severely because they are those of a tyro.

I must record my gratitude to Professor Edgar Wind for warning me of the dangers that beset my enterprise, for correcting a number of mistakes in the MS of my second lecture, and for making valuable positive suggestions, among which I would call particular attention to that recorded in the footnote on p. 67. If he was unable to dissuade me from my foolhardiness, his help will at least, I hope, have diminished the penalties I may be called upon to pay for it.

JOHN SPARROW

I

THE EVOLUTION OF THE INSCRIPTION

In this series of lectures I shall try briefly to describe the development of the inscription as a literary form. The subject is not quite so narrow or so trivial as it may sound; it embraces a strange and unrecorded episode in literary history: how in the seventeenth century a new taste spread all over Europe, a taste for books whose whole text took the form of an extended inscription or series of inscriptions; and it raises a curious question in aesthetics: how far the eye can play a part in the appreciation of a work of literature.

DEFINITION

In order to understand the story, we must be clear at the outset what we mean by 'an inscription'. In its widest and most literal sense the word covers anything written upon anything else, the verb 'written' implying not that the inscription must be traced with a pen—it may be printed, or cut on stone, or painted on pottery, or burnt into glass, or recorded in any other way—but that it must consist of *words*; neither patterns nor pictures can properly be classified as inscriptions.

This interpretation, clearly, is too wide for our purpose; it covers every manuscript that was ever written and every example of a printed book; when we talk about 'an inscription' we have in mind something belonging to a narrower class than that. What then is the characteristic of a piece of manuscript or print that qualifies it to be called, in ordinary parlance, an inscription? It is, I suggest, that it should comprise a sequence of words designed to be read with the eye.

True, everything that is written or printed is presumably intended to be read, and everything (if we except Braille) that is intended to be read is intended to be read with the eye—what else have we to read with? It is the peculiar characteristic of the inscription that it is specially and essentially intended for visual display.

Here we must distinguish between the inscription that is, in effect, no more than a public notice and the inscription that has pretensions to being a literary work. The examples that come most readily to mind when we think of 'an inscription' are inscriptions on tomb-stones or memorials or public buildings; these are in a sense public notices, put up for him who runs to read; they are not necessarily (though they may be) examples of literary art. Usually their texts are inscribed on stone for the sake of publicity or record; in classical and in mediaeval times, before the invention of printing, that was the best way of publishing a law or a proclamation if it was desired that large numbers of persons should become acquainted with its contents. It was set up in order to be seen by as many people as possible. But the 'literary' inscription makes a subtler appeal to the eye than that; its distinguishing feature is that those who become acquainted with its contents indirectly—say, by hearing it read aloud—and who do not see it, or at least envisage in their mind's eye the spatial arrangement of the text, will miss something of its full effect.

The peculiarity of this particular literary form is that the composer thinks in lines, the line-division being determined not by the requirements of metre or of an intended visual pattern, but by his desire to present what he has to say in a visual form that will bring his meaning clearly and fully home to the person who sees it. An inscription thus composed, if the typographer or carver who gives it actuality carries out the design of the composer, will produce by its lineation an effect on the person who sees it that it would fail to produce on someone who simply heard it read aloud.

A piece of prose or verse as ordinarily printed or set out, whether on paper or on stone, however much it pleases the eye by the beauty of its lettering or layout, does not fulfil the requirements of an inscription as a literary form. Neither verse nor prose is ordinarily printed in a form designed to enhance, by a planned division into lines, the meaning of the text.

With prose, the length of the lines is determined only by the breadth of the page on which the text is printed. Occasionally, where there is a marked break in the sense, there will be a division between paragraphs; but otherwise the text is solid; pauses and clauses are indicated by punctuation.

Verse, on the other hand, is normally printed in lines the length of which is

34   *The Church.*

¶ Eafter wings.

Lord, who createdft man in wealth and ftore,
Though foolifhly he loft the fame,
Decaying more and more,
Till he became
Moft poore:
With thee
O let me rife
As larks, harmonioufly,
And fing this day thy victories:
Then fhall the fall further the flight in me.

Eafter

The Church.   35

¶ Eafter wings.

My tender age in forrow did beginne:
And ftill with ficknefses and fhame
Thou didft fo punifh finne,
That I became
Moft thinne.
With thee
Let me combine,
And feel this day thy victorie:
For, if I imp my wing on thine,
Affliction fhall advance the flight in me.

H. Ba-

1. 'Easter Wings', from George Herbert's *The Temple*, 1633.

determined by the metre;[1] its form is designed not to please the eye but to help the ear.

Not all writing intended for the eye fulfils the conditions I have suggested as essential to the 'literary' inscription: a writer may 'lineate' his text in such a way as to obtain an effect that cannot be appreciated by someone who hears it read aloud, and yet not produce an inscription as I have defined it. Two familiar specimens of this kind of writing are the 'Easter Wings' of George Herbert (Plate 1) and the Mouse's Tale in *Alice in Wonderland* (Plate 2). Such

[1] It may, of course, be printed solid, like prose; verse was sometimes so presented in classical inscriptions.

so that her idea of the tale was something like
this :——"Fury said to
a mouse, That
he met in the
house, 'Let
us both go
to law: *I*
will prose-
cute *you*.——
Come, I'll
take no de-
nial: We
must have
the trial;
For really
this morn-
ing I've
nothing
to do.'
Said the
mouse to
the cur,
'Such a
trial, dear
sir. With
no jury
or judge,
would
be wast-
ing our
breath.'
'I'll be
judge,
I'll be
jury,'
said
cun-
ning
old
Fury:
'I'll
try
the
whole
cause,
and
con-
demn
you to
death'."

2. The Mouse's Tale, from Lewis Carroll's *Alice in Wonderland*, 1865.

'figured' writing goes back, as Herbert no doubt knew and Lewis Carroll perhaps did not know, to very early times; there are examples of it not only in late Latin literature but in late Greek literature also; the sixteenth and seventeenth centuries provide a rich crop of examples, and in the present century it was practised extensively by Guillaume Apollinaire. But though it has something in common with inscriptional writing—for the essential appeal is in both cases to the eye—writing of this kind is not inscriptional, because the visual form does not contribute to the meaning of the text, but merely illustrates it; such examples are simply a kind of visual pun.[1]

[1] The shape of a piece of writing may also be determined (*a*) by the desire of the printer or engraver to produce a pleasing pattern unrelated to the meaning of the text he is transcribing, or (*b*) by conformity to the shape of the stone or other surface on which it is inscribed.

A 'literary' inscription, then, is a text composed with a view to its being presented in lines of different lengths, the lineation contributing to or enhancing the meaning, so that someone who does not see it, actually or in his mind's eye, but only hears it read aloud misses something of the intended effect. Such inscriptions are examples of a literary form that differs both from verse and from prose as it is ordinarily composed and presented. That is what is meant in these lectures by the inscription as a literary form.[1]

CLASSICAL INSCRIPTIONS

Two Western cultures have produced inscriptions in profusion: Greece and Rome. Greece planted them on her own mainland, on the islands and shores of the Aegean, on the banks of the Nile, and, less profusely, in the Western Mediterranean. Rome scattered hers over the whole of the Western world. Most of these inscriptions—or, at least, most of those that have survived— were cut in stone, though texts were committed also to less durable materials.

Even in the fragmentary state in which they have come down to us— fragmentary, both because collectively they are but a small proportion of a much larger mass that must have perished and because individually many of them are but broken remnants—the thousands of inscriptions that have survived from ancient Greece and Rome constitute a rich treasury for students of antiquity. Classical inscriptions have been the subject of scientific study by the political and the economic historian, the historian of religion and of law, and the student of manners, as well as by the philologist. But such students, regarding inscriptions simply as historical evidence, have concentrated on their texts, paying regard to their script and their physical characteristics only in order to assign to them their proper date and provenance and so fit them into their historical context. Others have studied classical inscriptions as decorative elements in monuments or for the beauty of their lettering or as evidence for

[1] Of course the printer or the engraver may frustrate the intentions of the composer by presenting a carefully lineated inscription, or a piece of verse, in solid form, as if it were ordinary prose. In such cases one can restore a verse inscription to its proper form by paying due attention to the metre; similarly, one should be able to restore a de-formed prose inscription by perceiving what must have been the line-division intended by its composer.

Sometimes the converse occurs: in the sixteenth and seventeenth centuries, when the lineated inscription had become a familiar form, one occasionally comes across an inscription in which the engraver has broken up a piece of verse, with a view to epigrammatic effect, or simply in order to make a pleasing pattern, into long lines and short lines that bear no relation to the metre.

the evolution of scripts and alphabets. No one, however, so far as I know, has studied classical inscriptions as a kind of literature; nor is this surprising, for the Greeks and the Romans themselves never considered the inscription from this point of view: practically all their inscriptions were records for public display, of one kind or another, not literary compositions.

By far the greatest number of Greek pre-Christian public inscriptions are laws, treaties, and similar documents; their texts were almost always the work of official draftsmen, not of creative writers; they were inscribed on stone or bronze simply for the purposes of record and publicity; they were displayed like the Carriage of Goods Regulations posted up at a railway station or the Carriers Act in the hall of a Trust House hotel, and their texts were laid out with a view to easy legibility rather than to aesthetic effect (Plate 3).

As for Greek private inscriptions, most of them, whether pagan or Christian, were carved on votive offerings or memorials or grave-stones; these gave the composer more scope for literary art. But Greek epigraphists took little advantage of this, usually confining themselves, if the inscription was in prose, to the briefest particulars and one or another of a few traditional formulae. In verse, of course, composers of epitaphs expressed their feelings more freely and variously; but the division of a verse epitaph into lines, in cases where they stop short of the edge of the stone, is governed simply by the metre. Neither in prose nor in verse, therefore, did the Greek epigraphist compose his text with a view to its being set out in lines determined by their sense; and only a small proportion of surviving Greek inscriptions, public or private, are cut in a fine letter or laid out with an eye to recognisable effect.[1] How often, looking at Greek *stelae*, one is struck by the contrast between the beauty of the sculptured relief and the poverty—both in content and in presentation—of the inscription above or beneath it! (Plate 4).

Rome affords a vivid contrast, at any rate in the visual aspect of its epigraphy. The Roman stone-cutters produced inscriptions that have never been surpassed for the beauty of their lettering. And on special occasions the cutter

---

[1] Connoisseurs of Greek epigraphy will point to exceptions: in the 'stoichedon' inscriptions of classical times each letter was placed carefully below the corresponding letter in the preceding line and the lines are regularly of equal length (so that the effect is not unlike that of a crossword puzzle), and there are plenty of Greek inscriptions in which the names of the persons recorded and the offices they held are 'displayed' in separate lines; but, generally speaking, Greece cannot, to a modern eye, compete with Rome in the lettering of its inscriptions or the art with which they are presented.

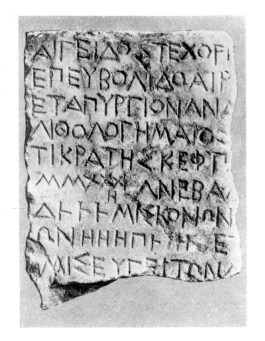

3. Attic inscriptions, early fourth century B.C.: (i) building accounts; (ii) list of ships' crews; (iii) regulations concerning sacrifices; (iv) decree of Athenian assembly (from J. Kirchner, *Imagines Inscriptionum Atticarum*, Berlin, 1948, Tafel 22).

7

4 (a). Stele of Ampharete,
Athens, c. 410 B.C. (Kirchner, Tafel 17).

4 (b). Monument of Dexileos,
Athens, 394/3 B.C. (Kirchner, Tafel 21).

5. Roman inscriptions, second to fourth centuries A.D.: *tituli* of persons of the senatorial and equestrian orders (from E. Diehl, *Inscriptiones Latinae*, Bonn, 1912, Tab. 18).

would pay attention to the presentation of his text, at any rate to the extent of giving prominence to an important name or title, and avoiding the division of a word between two lines.

But the men who cut most everyday Roman inscriptions were not adepts at their art; they had no eye for elegance, and they paid no regard to the content of their texts. They were concerned to save stone—an expensive material— and in ninety-nine cases out of a hundred they would fill the inscribed surface from side to side and from top to bottom, dividing words between lines, cramping words, abbreviating relentlessly, and diminishing the size of their letters in order to get them into the given space (Plate 5).

As for the composer, he did not usually design his text with a view to its visual presentation. Many, perhaps most, of the Roman inscriptions that have survived are, like their Greek counterparts, official documents that allow no scope for creative originality; and even where the epigraphist enjoyed greater freedom, as in epitaphs or *elogia*, he would not let himself go far beyond an enumeration of the offices held by the deceased, their campaigns, their triumphs, and the services they performed for their country; he would not shape his sentences with a view to lineated display. Epitaphs were sometimes composed in verse and funeral elegies were sometimes inscribed on sepulchral monuments;[1] but there the division into lines was determined by the metre and not by the requirements of the sense.

In short, the Romans did not regard the inscription as a literary form any more than did the Greeks.

POST-CLASSICAL AND MEDIAEVAL INSCRIPTIONS

The Dark Ages and the Middle Ages have little to show in the way of inscriptions in which either the text or its presentation can claim to be a work of art.

The Western prose inscription, from the fall of the Roman Empire until the middle of the fifteenth century, was usually factual or formulary; even in epitaphs, which allowed and indeed invited the expression of personal feeling, the text normally consisted of facts and dates, with or without a brief commendation of the person commemorated and a summary of his offices or achievements, preceded or followed by some such formula as 'Hic jacet' or 'Cuius animae propitietur Deus'. If the epigraphist wished to express his feelings in panegyric or elegy, he turned almost invariably to verse—to crude elegiacs or, more often, leonine hexameters. If he wrote in prose, he did not compose the text with a view to its being set out line by line; and the mediaeval stone-cutter rarely presented an inscription in lines of varying length: he usually filled a rectangular stone from edge to edge, regardless of the pauses or paragraphs demanded by the sense or the metre, or else he ran his inscriptions continuously round the rim of a tomb-slab or narrow architectural frieze, so that the opportunity for lineation simply did not exist (Plate 6).[2]

[1] Cf., for example, Suetonius, *De vita Caesarum*, v (Divus Claudius), i, 5; *Nec contentus (Augustus) elogium tumulo eius (sc. Decimi Drusi) versibus a se compositis insculpsisse, etiam vitae memoriam prosa oratione composuit.* The 'Tria epigrammata trium veterum poetarum, Naevii, Plauti, Pacuvii', that form the subject of Aulus Gellius, *Noctes Atticae*, i, xxiv, were in verse and, according to Gellius, 'sepulcris eorum incisa sunt'.

[2] Sometimes, working within the limits imposed by circumstances, the stone-cutter would spread himself, as far as the architecture of the day allowed, in inscriptions on a church front or under a statue. So, at the turn of the twelfth century, did Wiligelmo on the façade of the Duomo at Modena: he used a decent Roman letter, which he may actually have copied from a classical original.

10

6. Monument of Cardinal Guglielmo Fieschi: Rome, S. Lorenzo fuori le Mura, thirteenth century.

Scribes—to whom parchment was as precious as stone was to the mason—were equally parsimonious: the title-page came in with print and paper, and then slowly; so did the paragraph.

A glance at any comprehensive collection of late Roman and mediaeval inscriptions will reveal how poor in specimens of literary or visual art was the epigraphy of the Dark and Middle Ages.[1]

RENAISSANCE INSCRIPTIONS

In Italy in the fifteenth century the classical inscription was reborn. A passion for imitating and re-creating the classical past possessed the Italian humanists from the end of the fourteenth century onwards. Their own literature and their daily life, as well as their art and architecture, were coloured not only by their study of classical texts but also by their archaeological discoveries: poets and scholars shared with sculptors in the excitement roused by the newly found Laocoon. Their study of inscriptions, like their study of literary texts and works of art, helped the humanists to re-create the world of classical antiquity. Ciriaco of Ancona collected inscriptions with the same passion that impelled Poggio in his search for manuscripts, and Pirro Ligorio indulged the same taste in producing them. This theme was brilliantly treated by Saxl in his article 'The Classical Inscription in Renaissance Art and Politics'.[2] But I know of no study that is devoted to the influence of the classical inscription upon its Renaissance counterpart and that gives an account of how the rediscovery of classical inscriptions affected contemporary epigraphy.

First, and most obviously, it affected the visible form of the inscription, and in particular its lettering. Experts have analysed in detail the various letter-forms that reappeared, or first appeared, in print, in manuscript, and on stone, in Renaissance Italy; they have traced the history of calligraphic and epigraphic alphabets and related them to their classical Roman ancestors, showing how, as a result of the humanists' study of classical Roman capitals,

---

[1] E.g. the collection of Christian inscriptions contained in the *Dictionnaire d'Epigraphie Chrétienne*, 'Par M. X...' (Paris, 1852), which forms volumes 30 and 31 of Migne's *Nouvelle Encyclopédie Théologique*, or Paul Deschamps' well-illustrated *Etude sur la Paléographie des Inscriptions lapidaires de la fin de l'époque Mérovingienne aux dernières années du XIIe siècle* (Paris, 1929), an account of inscriptions from all over France from the eighth to the twelfth century.

[2] *Journal of the Warburg and Courtauld Institutes*, IV (1940–1), 19–46.

both in manuscript and on marble, stone-cutters began during the fifteenth century to use much more legible and shapely forms of letter, so that inscriptions acquired a new beauty.[1] This led designers of monuments to display them boldly instead of stringing them along narrow ledges or tucking them away on tablets that formed no part, or no important part, of their main design. The inscription-bearing tablet, with its fine display of lettering, was no longer an aesthetic irrelevance: it became an integral and prominent feature of the monument.

Meanwhile, the text itself had also begun to undergo a metamorphosis, and no doubt the change in content was connected with the change in visible form: in the middle of the fifteenth century the inscribed verse epitaph went completely out of fashion. Any one who has made even a superficial survey of Italian monuments must have received, consciously or unconsciously, the impression that this is so, and the truth of that impression is strikingly confirmed by statistics.

From St Peter to Pius XI, there were two hundred and sixty Popes.[2] No epitaphs survive for the first seventeen of them, nor for a hundred and ten others. Of the one hundred and thirty-three contemporary Papal epitaphs that have survived, either on stone or on paper, sixty-nine are metrical. *All sixty-nine are epitaphs of Popes who died before Pius II (1464)*; the epitaph of Nicholas V (d. 1455) was the last Papal epitaph to be written in verse. All the eighteen other pre-1464 Papal epitaphs were 'formulary'; that is to say, they consisted of little, if anything, more than names, titles, offices, and dates; the extended prose epitaph had not yet come into use on Papal monuments.[3]

After the disappearance of verse in the mid-fifteenth century, the extended prose epitaph prevailed for more than a hundred years: of the twenty-one Popes between Pius II (d. 1464) and Gregory XV (d. 1623), inclusive, whose

---

[1] I need only mention (in alphabetical order) Mrs Nicolette Gray, Dr Giovanni Mardersteig, Professor Millard Meiss, Mr Charles Mitchell, the late Stanley Morison, Mr James Mosley, and the late James Wardrop.

[2] I take my statistics from *Le Tombe dei Papi* by Renzo U. Montini (Rome, 1957). This excellent work prints the epitaphs, illustrates the monuments, and gives full bibliographical references. My figures must be taken subject to two warnings: it is not always possible to say how far an epitaph is 'contemporary' (i.e. how soon after the death of its subject it was composed), nor is it always possible to draw a clear line between the 'formulary' and the extended prose epitaph.

[3] Montini (*op. cit.* p. 46) classifies the epitaph of Clement V (d. 1314) as 'prose'; it seems to me no more than 'formulary'. It is probably contemporary with the erection of the Pope's monument in 1359 (Montini, pp. 247–8).

13

epitaphs have survived, eight were commemorated by formulary inscriptions; the remaining thirteen epitaphs were in extended prose.[1]

Since Gregory XV, an austerer practice has prevailed: of the twenty-five subsequent Popes down to (and including) Pius XI, only four (Clement IX, d. 1669; Clement XI, d. 1721; Clement XVI, d. 1774; and Leo XII, d. 1829) were accorded a full prose epitaph; the rest were formulary.

The same pattern displays itself in Venice. The earliest surviving contemporary epitaph of a Doge dates from the beginning of the twelfth century; twenty-one contemporary epitaphs survive of Doges dying during the following three hundred and fifty years; sixteen of these are in verse, and of the five others only one is more than formulary. Of the Doges dying after 1450 (and there were nearly fifty of them), not one was commemorated by an epitaph in verse.[2] Again, verse disappears in the middle of the fifteenth century and the extended prose epitaph comes into its own.

A survey of the epitaphs of Cardinals reveals the same trend over a wider field. I recently acquired a manuscript volume, prepared for the press in the mid-eighteenth century but never (so far as I know) printed, containing an apparently complete collection of the epitaphs of Cardinals from the earliest times.[3] It provides some interesting statistics. If its evidence is to be trusted (and it is reliable as far as I have been able to check it), just under one hundred and fifty contemporary epitaphs of Cardinals have survived from the end of the twelfth to the middle of the fifteenth century; sixty-three are in verse, fifty-three are in prose, and twenty-eight are formulary. The proportion of prose is higher than one might have expected; but after 1450 the same striking

---

[1] Gregory XV, who was responsible for the canonisation of S. Ignatius Loyola, was buried in S. Ignazio in Rome, in the same tomb as his nephew Cardinal Ludovico Ludovisi (d. 1632), who was responsible for the building of the church. The commemorative inscription on their joint tomb, with its phrase ALTER IGNATIVM ARIS ALTER ARAS IGNATIO, must be contemporary with the monument, which is the work of Pierre Le Gros the younger (1666–1719). The extended prose epitaph on Gregory (reprinted by Montini, *op. cit.* pp. 360–2, from *Ciaconius Vitae et res gestae Pontificum Romanorum et S.R.E. Cardinalium*, 2nd ed. Rome, 1677, IV, 470) was composed by G. B. Ursi, S.J., and is printed at p. 190 of his *Inscriptiones* (Naples, 1643); it was presumably written immediately after the death of its subject and inscribed on his 'deposito provvisorio'.

[2] I take these facts from A. Da Mosto, *I Dogi di Venezia* (Ongania, Venice, 1939), which contains transcriptions of the epitaphs of all the Doges and photographs of most, if not all, of their monuments.

[3] I transcribe the title-page, which in the MS is set out as if for the printer: *Nomina, Cognomina, Patriae, Dignitates, ac Tituli omnium San. Romanae Ecclae. Cardinalium, a quo Pontifice creati fuerunt, sub quo Pontifice decesserunt, et in qua Ecclesia sepulti fuerunt, cum sepulcralibus inscriptionibus, collecta a Cler. Io. Ant. Curtio Capace Romano Romae Anno Domini MDCCLVIIII.*

14

contrast presents itself: out of two hundred and fifty-five such epitaphs for the period 1450–1600, fewer than twenty are in verse; twenty-four consist of formulae, and two hundred and twelve are extended prose epitaphs.

There is preserved in Bologna a remarkable series of twenty-eight inscribed monuments to jurists who were *lettori* in the University.[1] Twenty-four of them belong to dates earlier than 1465 (they range from 1260 to 1439); of these twenty-four inscriptions, sixteen are in verse, and six of the remaining eight are formulary. None of the four post-1465 inscriptions is in verse; and on three of the earlier monuments an additional inscription has been engraved after 1450; all of these are in prose.

One can perceive the same pattern in the series of epitaphs of Kings, Emperors, Electors and illustrious persons contained in Parts I and II of *Theatrum Funebre*, a comprehensive collection of epitaphs compiled by Conrad Aicher and published at Salzburg in two stout quarto volumes in 1673 and 1675.[2]

It is plain, then, that in the middle of the fifteenth century the epitaph in verse was ousted from sepulchral monuments by the epitaph in prose.

Why, one naturally asks, should this have happened? It is not, I think, simply that the humanistic epigraphists were ashamed to copy the doggerel verses of their mediaeval predecessors. If they had wished to write sepulchral inscriptions in verse they could have written them in classical hexameters or elegiacs, as indeed they sometimes did.[3] But verse is very much the exception and prose the rule in monumental inscriptions of the Renaissance.

There were probably more reasons for this than one. In the Middle Ages, the composer was normally writing an elegy, without thinking of the stone to which it might subsequently be transferred; naturally, he wrote his elegy in verse. His verses were engraved on stone because that was the best means of preserving and publishing what he had written at a time when the printing press was not there to perform that function. The Renaissance epigraphist, on

---

[1] See Corrado Ricci, *Monumenti Sepolcrali di lettori dello studio bolognese nei secoli XIII, XIV, e XV* (Bologna, 1888).

[2] *Theatrum Funebre, Exhibens per varias scenas Epitaphia nova, antiqua, seria, jocosa...cum Summorum Pontificum, Imperatorum, et Regum Galliae, succincta Chronologia, eorumque Symbolis ac Epitaphiis, Extructum a Dodone Richea B.* In this collection contemporary epitaphs are mingled with later epitaphs and elegies, so that the pattern does not emerge very clearly.

[3] For instance, the epitaphs on the tombs of Marsuppini (1453) in Florence and Sannazaro (1530) in Naples.

IOANNES·ACVTVS·EQVES BRITANNICVS·DVX·AETATIS·S
VAE CAVTISSIMVS·ET·REI·MILITARIS PERITISSIMVS·HABITVS·EST
PAVLI·VCCELLI·OPVS·

7. Uccello, Monument of Sir John Hawkwood: Florence, Duomo, 1436.

the other hand, worked in close conjunction with the sculptor and the architect; he did not forget that his text was to be incorporated in a monument;
for such a purpose it was natural to write in prose.

Classical models, also, no doubt had their influence, in particular the prose
elogia that the Romans inscribed on tombs and memorials to illustrious
citizens, like the *elogia Scipionum* and the *tituli honorarii* that Augustus caused
to be inscribed on the bases of statues in the Forum. An early example is
provided by the fresco in the Duomo in Florence commemorating Sir John
Hawkwood, the famous English *condottiere*. Hawkwood died, in the service
of Florence, in 1393; the fresco, which represents an equestrian monument,
was executed by Uccello forty-three years later (Plate 7). For the lettering
of the inscription that he depicted upon the base of this monument, Uccello
had evidently taken lessons, if only elementary lessons, from the Romans; it
is to classical Rome also that he, or whoever composed the inscription for him,
had recourse for its text. Instead of writing leonine hexameters, or making use
of pious *formulae*, he took his *elogium* word for word from the inscription in
honour of Q. Fabius Maximus which had then recently been discovered at
Arezzo[1] and was subsequently copied into many Renaissance anthologies of
classical inscriptions:[2] *dux aetatis suae cautissimus et rei militaris peritissimus
habitus est.*[3]

Another example from Florence is Bernardo Rossellino's monument in
S. Croce of Leonardo Bruni (d. 1444; Plate 8). According to Mr John Pope-
Hennessy,[4] 'no Florentine tomb exercised so great an influence as the Bruni
monument'. One of its most striking features is the classical beauty of the
Roman lettering in the inscription; no less striking, and no less classical, is the
text:

---

[1] Saxl points out that S. A. Morcelli, in his *Opera Epigraphica* (Padua, 1819, I, 265), observes that Francesco
Barbaro borrows freely from this inscription for his epitaph on Erasmo Gattamelata.

[2] See *C.I.L.* XI, 1828. To the list there given of Renaissance MSS containing this inscription we may add
the collection made by Bartolomeo della Fonte: see Saxl's account of the Ashmole MS in the article
referred to at p. 12 above.

[3] In 1456 Andrea del Castagno was commissioned to execute a memorial in the Duomo of another
Florentine *condottiere*, Niccolò da Tolentino (d. 1435). Castagno's fresco is a companion piece to Uccello's
Hawkwood memorial; on the base of his frescoed statue he inscribed, in primitive capitals, a similar,
but simpler, set of words: HIC QVEM SVBLIMEM IN EQVO CERNIS NICOLAVS TOLENTINAS EST
INCLITVS DVX FLORENTINI EXERCITVS.

[4] *Italian Renaissance Sculpture* (Phaidon, 1958), p. 42.

POSTQVAM LEONARDVS E VITA MIGRAVIT
HISTORIA LVGET ELOQVENTIA MVTA EST
FERTVRQVE MVSAS TVM GRAECAS
TVM LATINAS LACRIMAS TENERE NON POTVISSE

Here again the composer, Carlo Marsuppini, has gone back to ancient Rome, and has actually turned verse into prose; his source is a verse epitaph on Plautus preserved by Aulus Gellius.[1]

It was the paganism of his inscription on the tomb of Isotta in S. Francesco at Rimini—D ISOTTAE ARIMINENSI B M SACRVM MCCCCL—that earned Sigismondo Malatesta a rebuke from Pius II: 'In eo templo', wrote the Pope, 'concubinae suae tumulum erexit et artificio et lapide pulcherrimum adiecto titulo gentili more in hunc modum, Divae Isottae sacrum.'[2] Pius took 'D' as the 'DIVAE' of classical inscriptions rather than the unclassical 'Dominae'; and in this, as Ricci points out,[3] he was interpreting it in accordance with what had become the fashion of the day.

The 'supreme example', according to Saxl,[4] of the 'neo-classic' style of epitaph is the inscription on the spot in S. Lorenzo where Cosimo de' Medici is buried, which consists simply of the words

COSMVS MEDICES
HIC SITVS EST
DECRETO PVBLICO PATER PATRIAE
VIX. AN. LXXV. MENS. III. DIES XX.

The inscriptions just quoted represent the first stage of Renaissance epigraphy, in which both the texts and their layout are closely copied from classical originals. For the first noteworthy breakaway, at least as regards text, we must turn from the Tempietto Malatestiano in Rimini to the Tempietto Pontaniano in Naples—the private chapel erected by the humanist scholar, poet, and man of affairs, Giovanni Gioviano Pontano, who was head of the literary academy that still bears his name.

[1] *Noctes Atticae*, I, xxiv, I (quoted from Varro, 'in libro de poetis primo'): 'postquam est mortem aptus Plautus, Comoedia luget, | scaena est deserta, dein Risus, Ludus, Iocusque | et Numeri innumeri simul omnes conlacrimarunt'.
[2] See C. Ricci, *Il Tempio Malatestiano* (1925), pp. 434–7.
[3] *Ibid.* p. 436.   [4] P. 23 of his article referred to at p. 12 above.

8. Bernardo Rossellino, Monument of Leonardo Bruni: Florence, S. Croce, 1444.

9. Tempietto Pontaniano: Naples, 1492.

In 1490 Pontano decided to build a memorial to his wife Hadriana, who had died earlier in that year. He had bought a plot of ground adjoining the Church of S. Maria Maggiore, and upon it he built a small rectangular chapel, which, on its completion in 1492, was dedicated to the Virgin and St John the Evangelist. The design was simplicity itself, and the chapel contained no sculpture or fresco or other decoration except a triptych over the altar and an elaborately tiled floor (Plate 9).[1]

[1] The architecture and contents of the chapel are fully described and its history is recounted by Riccardo Filangieri di Candida in a paper read to the Accademia Pontaniana and printed on pp. 103–39 of the volume of its Proceedings for 1926, 'Il Tempietto di Gioviano Pontano in Napoli'.

Pontano used this modest chapel to house a small collection of classical inscriptions that he had got together, and to provide a setting for certain memorial inscriptions that he composed for himself and members of his family.

The inscriptions with which Pontano filled his *tempietto* became famous. They were transcribed by visitors—Marcantonio Michiel sent copies to his friends in Venice in 1519—and they were included in several of the printed collections of inscriptions that appeared in the course of the sixteenth century.[1] In the succeeding century they were still a show-piece for travellers; John Evelyn records in his *Diary* a visit to the chapel, and makes particular reference to the inscriptions.[2]

While Pontano's inscriptions became celebrated, the chapel that contained them fell into neglect. When Philip d'Orville visited the place in the 1720s, he found it in a dilapidated state which he describes in a pleasing set of Latin iambics; it was no longer used as a chapel, and at the entrance a ragged tailor plied his trade.[3]

By the middle of the eighteenth century, Pontano's temple was in decay, and it was on the point of being pulled down when, in 1759, the King intervened and ordered its restoration.[4]

Since then, the passage of two hundred years has reduced Pontano's chapel to something like its old neglected state; it is now used for the secular purposes of a local confraternity, and the structure is in sad need of repair. But the inscriptions still survive. On the outside are twelve tablets, each bearing a Latin apophthegm composed by Pontano for the edification of his fellow citizens. Inside may be seen a small collection of classical inscriptions—two Greek, four Roman—and a short inscription marking the site of a most precious relic which has now, unfortunately, disappeared: an arm of the

[1] Several of them, for instance, are included in Apianus' *Inscriptiones Sacrosanctae Vetustatis* (1534); see below, p. 26 .

[2] February 1645; *Diary*, ed. de Beer (Oxford, 1955) II, 328–9. Evelyn's account of the chapel is based on J. H. von Pflaumern's *Mercurius Italicus* (1628), pp. 457–63, where all the inscriptions are printed.

[3] D'Orville's verses are printed by R. de Sarno in his Latin life of Pontano (Naples, 1761), pp. 102–5. De Sarno at p. 46 himself describes the state of the chapel a quarter of a century after d'Orville's visit: 'Proh rerum, temporumque vices!' he exclaims, 'tam praeclarum munificentiae Pontanianae, ejusque nominis monumentum, quod exteri sartum, tectumque in aevum voluissent, vel aetatis malignitate, vel curatorum parum sincera fide maxima annorum intercapedine situ squalidum, sentum, omnique religione desertum emarcuit, non sine doctissimorum hospitum ad illud invisendum longe gentium confluentium indignatione ad nostrum civium ludibrium.'

[4] The work was put in the charge of Giacomo Martorelli, who occupied the Chair of Greek at the University of Naples; see de Sarno, *op. cit.* pp. 42–6.

historian Livy, procured from Padua and bequeathed to Pontano by Antonio Beccadelli Panormitanus, the founder of the Accademia Pontaniana.

For the historian of post-classical epigraphy, the chief interest of the chapel lies in the series of inscriptions composed by Pontano to commemorate himself, his wife and children, and his friend Pietro Gulino. Three of these have for their subjects his sons—two, on separate tablets, record his grief for his favourite Lucio, who died at the age of twenty-nine in 1498; the third commemorates another Lucio, a son of his second marriage, who died in infancy. Moving though these are, they are not of particular epigraphical interest or importance; they are verse elegies, and they were included, with slight textual variants, among Pontano's published poems. The tablets put up in memory of his wife and his daughter, on the other hand, are inscribed not only with elegiac verses, but with prose epitaphs, which were composed especially to be engraved upon the memorial stone. These epitaphs, and those that Pontano composed for himself and for Gulino, 'il Compatre', are so remarkable that they deserve to be set out here in full.

Here is the inscription on the tomb of Hadriana:

QVINQVENNIO POSTQVAM VXOR ABIISTI
DEDICATA PRIVS AEDICVLA
MONVMENTVM HOC TIBI STATVI
TECVM QVOTIDIANVS VT LOQVERER

NEC SI MIHI NON RESPONDES
NON RESPONDEBIT DESIDERIVM TVI
PER QVOD IPSA MECVM SEMPER ES
AVT OMMVTESCET MEMORIA
PER QVAM IPSE TECVM NVNC LOQVOR

HAVE IGITVR MEA HADRIANA
VBI ENIM OSSA MEA TVIS MISCVERO
VTERQVE SIMVL BENE VALEBIMVS

VIVENS TECVM VIXI ANNOS XXIX DIES XXIX
VICTVRVS POST MORTVVS
AETERNITATEM AETERNAM

and here is the inscription in which Pontano mourns his daughter:

MVSAE FILIA LVXERVNT TE IN OBITV
AT LAPIDE IN HOC LVGET TE PATER TVVS
QVEM LIQVISTI IN SQVALORE CRVCIATV GEMITV

HEV HEV FILIA
QVOD NEC MORIENTI PATER AFFVI
QVI MORTIS CORDOLIVM TIBI DEMEREM
NEC SORORES
INGEMISCENTI QVAE COLLACRIMARENTVR MISELLAE
NEC FRATER SINGVLTIENS
QVI SITIENTI MINISTRARET AQVVLAM
NON MATER IPSA
QVAE COLLO IMPLICITA ORE ANIMVLAM EXCIPERET
INFELICISSIMA
HOC TAMEN FELIX
QVOD HAVD MVLTOS POST ANNOS TE REVISIT
TECVMQVE NVNC CVBAT
AST EGO FELICIOR
QVI BREVI CVM VTRAQVE EDORMISCAM
EODEM IN CONDITORIO

VALE FILIA
MATRIQVE FRIGESCENTI CINERES INTERIM CALFACE
VT POST ETIAM REFOCILLES MEOS

It would be hard to find anything quite like these inscriptions on any gravestone of classical Rome, still more on any mediaeval or fifteenth-century sepulchral monument. They are prose poems, in which the composer's emotions are expressed in words which presuppose that the text is to be inscribed on a memorial; yet, though they are in a sense intended for monumental display, they would not achieve their full effect if they were subordinated to the design of a sculptor or monumental mason; they are evidently meant to stand by themselves on a plain floor-slab or mural tablet.

Scarcely less remarkable, though in a different vein, are the epitaphs Pontano composed for himself and for his friend Gulino. Here is his own epitaph:

VIVVS DOMVM HANC MIHI PARAVI

IN QVA QVIESCEREM MORTVVS

NOLI OPSECRO INIVRIAM MORTVO FACERE

VIVENS QVAM FECERIM NEMINI

SVM ETENIM

IOANNES IOVIANVS PONTANVS

QVEM AMAVERVNT BONAE MVSAE

SVSPEXERVNT VIRI PROBI

HONESTAVERVNT REGES DOMINI

SCIS IAM QVI SIM

AVT QVI POTIVS FVERIM

EGO VERO TE HOSPES NOSCERE IN TENEBRIS NEQVEO

SED TEIPSVM VT NOSCAS ROGO

VALE

and here is the Gulino inscription:

QVID AGAM REQVIRIS?

TABESCO

SCIRE QVIS SIM CVPIS?

FVI

VITAE QVAE FVERINT CONDIMENTA ROGAS?

LABOR DOLOR AEGRITVDO LVCTVS

SERVIRE SVPERBIS DOMINIS

IVGVM FERRE SVPERSTITIONIS

QVOS CAROS HABEAS SEPELIRE

PATRIAE VIDERE EXCIDIVM

NAM VXORIAS MOLESTIAS NVNQVAM SENSI

Like his apostrophes to his wife and daughter, these epitaphs of Pontano's were plainly intended to be inscribed upon the stone of a memorial. But I doubt whether, when he composed them, Pontano thought in lines; and, like the rest of the inscriptions in his chapel, whether in verse or in prose, they were set out (no doubt at his own direction) in the manner of ancient Roman

24

inscriptions, with no space between words and in lines that reach uniformly to the edge of the stone and end, if need be, in the middle of a word.

And yet Pontano's inscriptions were not conceived by him as passages of ordinary prose: the apostrophes to his wife and daughter were, as I have said, really prose poems; their force and feeling, like the epigrammatic force of the two epitaphs, come through more effectively if they are broken up and presented in 'lineated' form, as I have printed them in the text.

Pontano's epitaphs mark the stage that the prose inscription had reached by the end of the fifteenth century; it was for the epigraphists of the sixteenth to exploit the possibilities of the lineated lapidary inscription, and for their successors in the seventeenth to transfer it from stone to paper.

PRINTED COLLECTIONS OF INSCRIPTIONS

The sixteenth century saw the emergence of a new type—or, one may say, two new types—of book: the collection of classical, and the collection of contemporary, inscriptions.

It was not until almost the end of the first quarter of the century that any of the manuscript collections of classical inscriptions made by the humanist scholars found its way into print. The first considerable printed collection was *Epigrammata Antiquae Urbis*, a small but splendid folio of some four hundred pages, edited and printed in Rome in 1521 by Giacomo Mazochi. As its title indicates, this volume includes only inscriptions found in Rome; its contents are arranged according to the region of the city where they were discovered. The book was four years in the press, and Mazochi took the opportunity provided by this interval to check all the inscriptions scrupulously. The results of his revision, including a number of minute *corrigenda*, are recorded in fourteen closely packed pages of *errata*, which, so far from proving (as has been suggested) his negligence, show what a careful and conscientious recorder he was. Mazochi makes some attempt to reproduce the layout of his originals, and he does not deck them out with fancy settings or imaginary backgrounds.

In his dedication, Mazochi claims that this is the first collection of its kind, or indeed the first attempt at any such collection: he is invading, he says, 'prouinciam quam aggredi, nedum perficere, nemo hactenus sit ausus'. But in fact he had himself, in 1510, published an anthology of some seventy inscriptions, which had been completed five years before by Francesco Albertini, 'qui primus omnium fuit, cui in mentem venit in lucem proferre typis expressa marmora vetustis litteris consignata'.[1] And earlier still, in 1505, Conrad Peutinger of Augsburg had published a smaller collection, a second edition of which appeared in 1520.[2]

It was Peutinger, with the collaboration and pecuniary assistance of Raimund Fugger, Willibald Pirckheimer and others, who supplied much of the material for the second great printed collection of classical inscriptions, *Inscriptiones Sacrosanctae Vetustatis*, which was published at Ingoldstadt in 1534 by Petrus Apianus and Bartolomaeus Amantius, professors in that University. This curious production was printed with specially cut types, the text of each page was encased in elaborate wood-cut borders, and the inscriptions were frequently presented in imaginary architectural settings. The book is famous for these typographical peculiarities, for its illustrations, and for the strange wood-cut after Dürer, on its title-page. It claims to supplement Mazochi by printing inscriptions from Spain, Germany, Africa, Greece, and Asia, besides the whole of Italy: 'Vetustatis', says the full title, 'non illae quidem Romanae sed totius fere orbis'.[3] It at least justifies Gori's assertion that Germany may contend with Italy 'de gloria primatus in edendis antiquis scriptis Marmoribus'.[4]

Mazochi, in his *Epigrammata Antiquae Urbis*, and Apianus, in his *Inscriptiones Sacrosanctae Vetustatis*, were each of them attempting to form a *corpus* of classical inscriptions; they were forerunners of Gruter, Smetius, Reinesius, and Scipio Maffei—and, ultimately, of Hübner, Mommsen, and the editors of the *Inscriptiones Graecae*. Their work was intended to help in the task of bringing to life again the world of ancient Rome and linking it with the world of the Renaissance.

In the middle of the sixteenth century a quite different kind of epigraphical collection began to win popularity—the collection of contemporary, or at least 'modern', inscriptions. Books of this kind ministered to a new range of tastes and interests, not classical, but literary and historical. Sometimes inscriptions were collected for their intrinsic beauty, sometimes for their association with a particular town or district; while sometimes (but this was a seven-

---

[1] See A. F. Gori, *Inscriptiones Antiquae in Etruriae Urbibus Exstantes*, Pars tertia (Florence, 1743), p. xxii.
[2] Gori, *loc. cit.*
[3] Apianus includes a few modern inscriptions—e.g. Pontano's epitaph on his wife Hadriana (see above, p. 22). [4] *Op. cit.* p. xxv.

teenth-century development) a publisher would assemble the productions of a particular composer.

Local collections were not common in Italy, or indeed elsewhere in Europe, in the sixteenth century;[1] and in the next century they seem to have been less popular in Italy than in countries north of the Alps.[2] They ministered to regional feeling, to civic sense, to antiquarian curiosity, to family pride. If we are looking for light on changes in taste or literary outlook, we should turn rather to collections made on a national or international scale.

It was in the mid-1550s that Lorenz Schrader, a boy of eighteen, set out from Halberstadt to visit Italy. He stayed three years, transcribing, simply out of curiosity, all the inscriptions he came across. He was without archaeological or ecclesiastical bias, and he did not confine himself to epitaphs. On his return, distinguished scholars—among those he mentions are Melanchthon, Camerarius, and Fabricius of Chemnitz—urged him to arrange and publish his finds. In 1567 he re-visited Italy, brought his collection up to date, and prepared it for the press. But he delayed publication—he was distracted, he tells us, by professional business—and, as the years went by, his collection again became out of date, and he had to employ what we should call a 'research assistant' ('proprium', as he puts it, 'alui studiosum') to fill in gaps among the earlier examples and to carry on his survey 'usque ad annum XCI'. Next year, in 1592, his book, *Monumentorum Italiae...Libri Quattuor*, came out at Helmstadt in a folio of medium size.

Schrader was interested in Christian, not pagan, and modern, not ancient, monuments; according to its title, the *Monumenta* comprised in it are those 'quae hoc nostro saeculo et a Christianis posita sunt'; it is the first comprehensive collection, covering the whole peninsula, of modern Italian inscriptions. It is a thoroughly German production, accurate, comprehensive, systematic, uninspired. Schrader does not reproduce the layout of the inscriptions or describe the monuments that carry them; but his is the first book of its kind, and it is of value for its comprehensiveness and because it records the text of many inscriptions that have since disappeared.

While Schrader was visiting Italy, a fellow-countryman of his was also

[1] The earliest Italian collection of the kind that I have discovered is di Stefano's census of Neapolitan inscriptions, published in 1560.

[2] I note the following local collections: Brabant (1613); Basel (1622, with supplement in 1661); Augsburg (1624); Wittenberg (1655); Hamburg (1663).

going on his travels. This was Siegfried Rybisch, a Silesian nobleman, Chancellor of the Exchequer to the Emperor Maximilian II. Rybisch was evidently a man of taste and energy; his travels were more extensive than Schrader's; his eye was keener and his taste more selective. From his youth, according to his publisher, he was inspired 'incredibili pietate et cognoscendarum historiarum atque Antiquitatum singulari quodam et ingenito amore et studio', and his delight lay in seeking out 'virorum praecipue ingenio et doctrina excellentium et tam prisci quam nostri saeculi memorabilium hominum monumenta cum Epitaphiis et inscriptionibus eruditis arte ingenioque elaborata atque exornata, ut quaeque vel antiquissima vel argutissima conquiri aut investigari potuerunt'.

'Antiquissima vel argutissima': historic or personal interest and literary or artistic quality were the qualities that Rybisch most valued, and he welcomed old and new alike. He was not content with copying the inscriptions: he made, or procured (it is not clear whether he employed artists), drawings of the monuments themselves.

In the 1570s, Rybisch made his collection of monumental drawings available to one Tobias Fendt, an engraver of Breslau, and allowed him to engrave them on copper and publish them in a single folio volume, which appeared in that city in 1574 (Plate 10).[1] Rybisch's interests being mainly artistic, Fendt's plates were not accompanied by any text, and he gives only the barest indication of where the monuments are to be found or whom they commemorate.

The first edition of this book contains a hundred and twenty-nine plates depicting rather more than a hundred and fifty inscriptions. A brief summary will give an idea of the variety and distinction of its contents. The first dozen plates display the epitaphs of classical writers, from Naevius to Papinian, with Sannazaro's monument thrown in to pair with Virgil's tomb at Posilippo; then come a dozen Northern humanists and reformers, including Erasmus, Conrad Celtes, Oecolampadius, and Melanchthon; then there are twenty plates illustrating the monuments of Petrarch, Dante, and Italian humanists—Politian, Valla, Bessarion, Pico—a series ending with Paolo Giovio, who died

[1] Its full title is *Monumenta Sepulcrorum cum Epigraphis Ingenio et Doctrina Excellentium Virorum: Aliorumque tam prisci quam nostri saeculi memorablium Hominum: De Archetypis expressa. Ex liberalitate Nob. et Clariss. Viri D. Sigefridi Rybisch &c. Caesarei Consiliarii. Per Tobiam Fendt, Pictorem et civem Vratislaviensem, in aes incisa et aedita.* Anno Chr. MDLXXIIII.

10. Title-page of Tobias Fendt's *Monumenta Excellentium Virorum* (Breslau, 1574).

in 1552. Nine plates are then devoted to the inscriptions in Pontano's *tempietto*. The next important group consists of no less than thirty plates, all of them depicting monuments in Bologna, some of them to humanists, others to mediaeval doctors of law. The last thirty-five plates are devoted not to monuments but to classical (or pseudo-classical) inscriptions; Fendt reproduces fifty-six of these, thirty-eight of them from originals that were found in Rome.

Fendt's *Monumenta* was evidently a success with the public for whom it was intended; in 1585 a second, and in 1589 a third, edition was published by Sigismund Feierabendt at Frankfurt, from the same plates but with a new engraved title-page by Jost Amman. Half a century later the same plates (the engraved title being suitably amended) did duty for a fourth edition at Amsterdam ('Apud Joannem Jansonium', 1638). In this edition, which was undertaken by the Dutch scholar Marcus Zuerius Boxhorn, most of the monuments were accompanied by *elogia* collected from other authors or composed by the editor and printed on the pages facing the plates; the title of the book was accordingly altered to *Monumenta Illustrium Virorum, et Elogia*.

That was not the end of the series. In 1671 there appeared at Utrecht an 'editio nova' of Boxhorn's *Monumenta…et Elogia*, '*Aucta Antiquis Monumentis in Agro Trajectino repertis*'. The identical plates were once more reproduced, with the addition of a comprehensive index and two plates representing inscriptions recently discovered in the neighbourhood and belonging to J. G. Graevius.

Fendt's book was an elaborate production, and it must have been expensive to buy; the fact that such a book maintained its popularity for a hundred years, and that the plates were made use of by publishers in four different and distant places, shows how strong and how widespread a taste for *monumenta* had grown up in the sixteenth century.

Fendt's *Monumenta* had its cheaper counterpart in another kind of book, of which the best example is the *Variorum in Europa Itinerum Deliciae* of Nathan Chytraeus (1543–98), professor of poetry at Rostock. The title-page of Chytraeus' book (Plate 11) sufficiently indicates its contents: its range covered all Europe, and it contained inscriptions of every kind, verse and prose, ancient and modern; but it made no attempt at being exhaustive, it was not the product of original research, but was drawn from manuscript and printed

11. Title-page of Nathan Chytraeus' *Variorum in Europa
Itinerum Deliciae* (3rd edn, Herborn, 1606).

sources, and it was produced, as the word *Deliciae* suggests, purely for the
amusement of its readers.

In the preface to his collection, Chytraeus gives a long list of the contributors
to whom he was indebted for its contents. He says that Schrader's *Monumenta*
came out when he was on the point of sending his own book to the press, and
that he took from it a number of inscriptions from Italy.[1]

[1] Chytraeus' *Deliciae* appeared in 1593, and was popular enough to reach a third edition ten years later.

Chytraeus' title was imitated by Franz Sweerts of Antwerp (1567–1629) for his *Selectae Christiannae Orbis Deliciae* (Cologne, 1608). Sweerts, like Chytraeus, was (as he confessed) only a compiler, making free use of Schrader, Chytraeus, and Fendt, who are among the eighty authorities to whom he acknowledges his indebtedness.

Sweerts's justification for publishing his *Deliciae* was that existing collections contained much that was heretical, so that they were barred from Catholic countries: 'quo fiebat ut ab Italia, illa insigni avitae Religionis parente, ab Hispania, Fidei veteris propugnatrice acerrima, aliisque locis Catholicis ceu contagiosae pestes exularent'.

Sweerts published his collection simply, he declared, in order to give pleasure: people who like only old inscriptions—'antiquas et intervallo temporum obsoletas marmorum Inscriptiones, Epitaphia, Cenotaphia, alia-que eiusmodi iam pene corrosa'—can betake themselves, he says, to Apianus and Amantius, to Smetius and Scaliger, to Velserus and Gruter and Justus Lipsius, where, he adds, they will be lucky if they find anything as delightful as the inscriptions produced by contemporary composers.[1]

While this activity was taking place on the Continent, England was lagging about a century behind, both in the production of inscriptions and in the production of books about them. The first Englishman to publish anything to compare with these Continental collections was Camden, who put out anony-mously in London in 1600 a small quarto catalogue of the epitaphs in West-minster Abbey.[2] This was simply a guide-book for the use of visitors, with translations of most of the Latin verse inscriptions into English verse—the sort of thing that today can be procured in a Cathedral from the verger, or is exposed for sale on a stall at the West door.

Indeed, there is evidence that Camden's book was offered to visitors to the Abbey in just this manner. In 1618 there was published in Frankfurt a duo-decimo volume entitled *Mausolea Regum, Reginarum, Dynastarum, Nobilium,*

---

[1] In 1625 appeared a second and enlarged edition of Sweerts's *Deliciae*, dedicated to Cardinal Francesco Barberini, nephew of Pope Urban VIII. Sweerts produced also *Epitaphia Ioco-Seria* (Cologne, 1623, 1645) and *Monumenta Sepulchralia et Inscriptiones Publicae Privataeque Ducatus Brabantiae* (Antwerp, 1613).

[2] *Reges, Reginae, Nobiles, Et alii in Ecclesia Collegiata B. Petri Westmonasterii sepulti.* Further, enlarged, editions appeared in 1603 and 1606.

Sumtuosissima, Artificiossima, Magnificentissima, Londini Anglorum In Occidentali urbis angulo structa. Its author was a certain Valens Arithmaeus, who tells us that he acted as tutor ('Achates fidus, aut Chiron') to a young nobleman of the family of Zedlitz, accompanying him on his travels, which lasted three years. Arithmaeus was particularly impressed by Westminster Abbey. He was so struck by the monuments that he decided to copy out the inscriptions on all of them—not quite such a labour of Hercules then as it would be today. But, he says, when the verger ('aeditimus et νεωκόρος') observed this, 'obtulit exemplar inscriptionum aliquot, ante multos annos excusarum', asking for it ('ex more gentis') a huge price. Arithmaeus bargained with him, and presumably got it cheap because he was sharp enough (he says) to observe that it omitted many of the more recent and more distinguished epitaphs; he added these himself to his copy of the book, 'volante nec errante calamo', and when he returned home negotiated with a publisher to bring out in print the augmented collection.

In fact, Arithmaeus' book is a reproduction of Camden's, omitting the English translations and adding several epitaphs, including that of Mary Queen of Scots, and transcripts of the epitaphs in St Paul's.

Arithmaeus in his preface exaggerated the importance of the additions he made to Camden's collection; but he was surely right when he said that the epitaphs are poor works of art, compared with the monuments on which they are inscribed—'Censuram vero non fero de inscriptionum mellificio, commendo lapicidarum artificium'.

The only English book of the period that compares in scale with contemporary Continental productions is John Weever's well-known *Ancient Funerall Monuments*, a folio of nearly 900 pages, which came out in 1631 (Plate 12).

Weever set out to do for Great Britain something like what Schrader did for Italy; like Schrader he travelled in search of inscriptions and based his copies on collections that he made himself.

Weever's book, however, does not fulfil the promise of its title-page; so far from covering 'the united Monarchie of Great Britaine, Ireland, and the Ilands adiacent', it deals only with the dioceses of Canterbury, Rochester, London, and Norwich. In his Epistle to the Reader, Weever announced his intention 'To publish to the view of the world, as well the moderne, as the ancient, memorialls of the dead throughout all his Maiesties foresaid

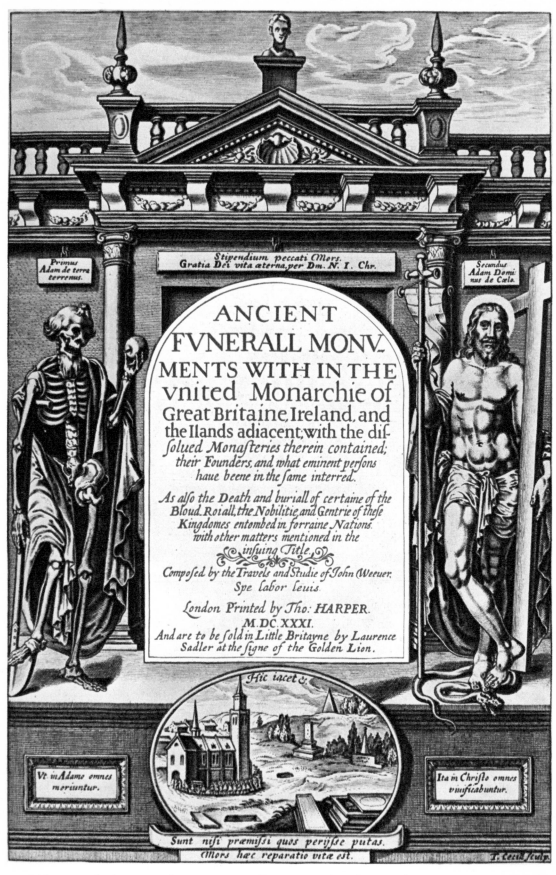

12. Title-page of John Weever's *Ancient Funerall Monuments* (London, 1631).

Dominions, if God spare me life'; but he died in the year following the publication of his book, and his undertaking remained imperfect.

Weever's phrase, 'as well the moderne, as the ancient', indicates the bent of his mind; though he included more recent specimens, it was the archaic that most interested him; his book is of a quite different kind from Schrader's; it was compiled with a different purpose in mind and to please a different public. Weever was an antiquarian in the tradition of Leland. He tells us that he would never have published his collections if it had not been for the encouragement of the Windsor Herald and Keeper of the Records in the Tower, Augustin Vincent, who gave him access to the records in the Herald's Office and introduced him to Sir Robert Cotton, to whom, together with Spelman, Selden, and Sir Simonds D'Ewes, he acknowledges his indebtedness.

Weever prefixes to his text a long 'Discourse of Funerall Monuments, &c' which contains a mass of ecclesiastical history, genealogy, and general antiquarianism; in his text he rarely records a monument much less than a century old. For a real English counterpart to Schrader we have to wait for the publication, at the beginning of the eighteenth century, of Le Neve's *Monumenta Anglicana*.

Yet Weever acknowledges as his forerunners 'Schraderus, Chytraeus, Swertius, and other forraine Writers', and his consciousness of his descent from them can be picturesquely demonstrated by setting the engraved title-page of his book[1] beside that of the *Monumenta Augustana* of Daniel Prasch, published at Augsburg in 1624 (Plate 13). But one has only to compare a couple of pages from their texts to see how different were their contents (Plates 14, 15). Prasch's text, with its carefully lineated epitaphs, shows the state that epigraphy had reached in the sixteenth century: it was no longer a branch of archaeology, no longer a branch of monumental design: it was an art and science of its own; people had become interested in inscriptions for their own sake, and that interest had created a new field not only for the stone-cutter but for the literary artist.

[1] His engraver was Thomas Cecil, who had engraved the title of Weever's first publication more than thirty years before.

STIPENDIVM . PECCATI . MORS :
GRATIA.DEI.VITA. AE TERNA.PER DN.N.I.CHR.

EPITAPHIA
AVGVSTANA
VINDELICA
AB.ANNIS.FERE..SEXCENTIS
VSQ AD.NOSTRAM.AETATEM
CONQVISITA
LABORE.ET.IMPENSIS
DANIELIS.PRASCHII
SALISBVRG-HALENSIS
Apud Brunonem Smitz Bibliopol.Aug.
ANNO.ORBIS.RED
M·DCXXIV.

PRIMVS ADAM
DE TERRA
TERRENVS

SECVND.ADAM
DOMINVS
DE COELO

VTI
IN. ADAMo
OMNES
MORI.
VNTVR

ITA
IN.CHRO
OMNES
VIVIFICA·
BVNTVR

MORS. HAEC REPARATIO VITAE. EST.

Wolf. Kilian. fcalp.

13. Title-page of Daniel Prasch's *Monumenta Augustana* (Augsburg, 1624).

15. Daniel Prasch's *Monumenta Augustana*, pp. 132–3.

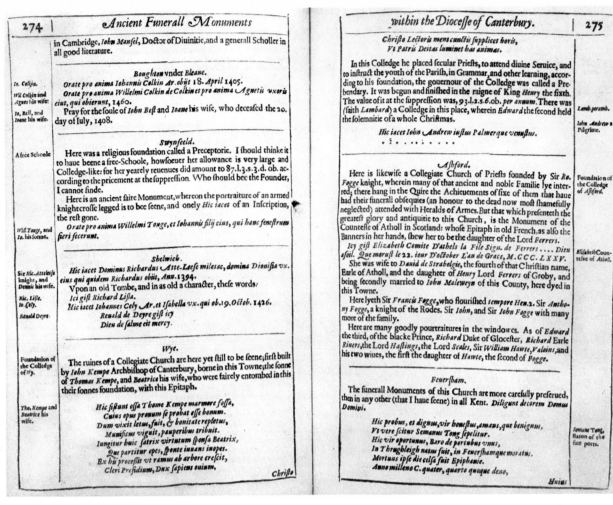

14. John Weever's *Ancient Funerall Monuments*, pp. 274–5.

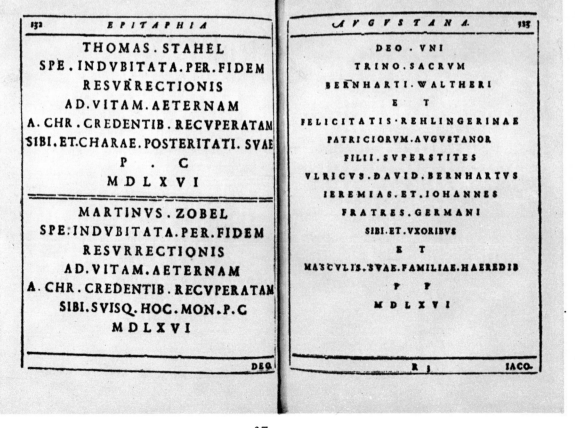

THE INSCRIPTION IN
RENAISSANCE WORKS OF ART

THE INSCRIPTION IN ARCHITECTURE

The passionate interest in epigraphy that the discovery of classical inscriptions aroused in educated men at the time of the Renaissance affected not only scholars and writers but also architects, painters, sculptors, and designers of monuments, all of whom testified to its strength by incorporating inscriptions in their work.

This epigraphical passion affected one art in one way, another in another. Architects and sculptors had only to transfer, as it were, to their own works, with more or less modification, what they saw inscribed upon buildings and monuments surviving from classical times. When a painter, on the other hand, incorporated in his picture a written text, more influences than one may have been at work upon him: sometimes, like the architect, he was making use of newly discovered classical material; sometimes he was following a tradition that had its roots in early Christian art.

In Renaissance Italy, the Latin inscription was ubiquitous. Perhaps the most striking testimony to its omnipresence in the mid-fifteenth century is the *Hypnerotomachia* of Francesco Colonna, in which imaginary inscriptions modelled on the antique occur on almost every other page. The inscription must have been an element in the background of the life of educated people at that time as insistent as the poster advertisement in the background of every-body's life today. Only a small proportion of that great crop of epigraphy has survived; but, even now, no one who has walked with his eyes open about the streets and squares of Italy and explored its churches and its *palazzi* can have failed to be impressed by the profusion of inscriptions with which the architects of the fifteenth and succeeding centuries adorned both the external and the internal faces of their buildings. Apart from the innumerable inscribed memorials with which the surface of so many Renaissance buildings became encrusted, the inscription was often an element in the architect's original design. The purpose for which a building was intended, the date when it was put up, the Saint to whom it was dedicated, the patron who paid for it—such particulars were very frequently recorded in lucid capitals on its façade.

The practice extended to interiors as well as to exteriors, and to civil and domestic as well as to ecclesiatical architecture. In the Palazzo del Te at Mantua, for instance, texts in fine Roman lettering were cut in marble over the fire-places and on the lintels of the door-ways, to please the eyes of the people who lived there and to give them something to think of, and perhaps to talk about; over a door-way in the Castello Sforzesco at Milan—the door led, presumably, to a dungeon or a treasury—are the words ABITE CLAVES ADVLTERINAE; phrases of welcome—NIL TECTI SVB TECTO and HOSPES NON HOSPES— are inscribed on the façade of the Villa Maser, while in the interior appropriate mottoes—IGNEM NE GLADIO FERIAS and IGNEM IN SINV NE AB- SCONDAS—adorn the chimney-pieces.

Architectural inscriptions were not so common in the Middle Ages. Gothic, in particular, with its aspiring arches and its avoidance of flat surfaces, of rectangular spaces and of horizontal lines, does not lend itself to epigraphy; a classical inscription, like that on the façade of the Duomo in Milan, fits uneasily into a Gothic setting; a text in Gothic script, on the other hand, is not easily read at a distance, and is, moreover, liable to be lost in the decora-tion that surrounds it. The prevalence of the Gothic style may help to explain why inscriptions absented themselves for so long from English architecture, hardly making an appearance until our builders began to take lessons from Vitruvius and Palladio.

An architect who wishes to embody an inscription in his work, whether as pure ornament or for the sake of what it says, is limited in his range of possible effects. He can use script to enliven a dead space on a wall (modern examples are to be found in Coventry Cathedral and at the west end of the chapel of Trinity College, Cambridge), or to ornament a frieze with a pattern at once continuous and unrepetitive (like Alberti's inscription round the Holy Sepulchre in the Rucellai Chapel in S. Pancrazio in Florence); and of course his letters may delight us (as do Alberti's) with a beauty of their own. But he can hardly do more than this with an inscription in order to give pleasure to the eye.

39

A Latin inscription, however, besides pleasing the eyes of those who look at it, may at the same time affect their emotions, and it may do this even if they do not understand what it means; it can, by its associations, convey a sense of grandeur—a sense, usually, of 'the grandeur that was Rome'. When we see a series of fine Roman letters carved on an entablature we feel, even if their actual meaning is obscure to us, that it is somehow fitting that classic words should adorn a classic structure; they minister, like a Latin grace in a college hall, to our sense of the appropriate—a sense that may derive pleasure even from simulated letters disposed in an apt setting.

It is not so easy for an architect to intensify the emotional impact of his work by means of the actual significance of words written on its face. Yet this too can be done. VENIET SICVT FVR is said to have been inscribed over the portals of the old Newgate Prison—an admonition that must, in the eyes of any malefactor who understood Latin and remembered the Bible, have appreciably added to the impressiveness of the façade. But a building cannot speak to us as articulately, or at as great a length, as can a monument or a memorial; the texts that form an integral part of its design must, from the very nature of the case, be short and simple. None the less, Renaissance architects did from time to time use the inscription as a means of contributing, not merely by the beauty of its lettering or by its general impressiveness, but by the actual message of its text, to the total effect that their work was intended to produce on the spectator. They sometimes used the inscription as a means, in their own phrase, of 'animating' their architectural structures.

Perhaps the most splendid example of this device is to be seen in Rome. 'Its noblest manifestation', says Mr James Mosley (he is referring to the tradition of lettering established by Giovanni Francesco Cresci), 'must surely be the great mosaic inscription, black on gold, which runs in a continuous band round the entablature of the Basilica of St Peter, and round the base of the cupola. The scale of this inscription—it is about 150 feet above the ground, and each letter must be fully 5 feet high—and its sturdy construction make this one of the grandest of all architectural letters.'[1] It is not only the lettering of the inscription that is impressive: the scriptural texts embodied in its gigantic capitals extend themselves along the whole length of the nave and transepts, to

[1] 'Trajan Revived', in *Alphabet* (1964), p. 28. Mr Mosley is concerned with the beauty and effectiveness of the lettering itself, rather than with the total effect of the inscription and its placing.

culminate with magnificent effect in the words TV ES PETRVS under the dome. 'Lo, yonder inscription', wrote Clive Newcome in his letter from Rome, 'which blazes round the dome of the Temple, so great and glorious it looks, like heaven almost, and as if the words were written in stars it proclaims to all the world that this is Peter, and on this rock the Church shall be built against which Hell shall not prevail.'

If Rome offers us the most superb example of an inscription 'animating' a Renaissance building, it is to Venice that we must go for the most elaborate. The façades of the great Venetian churches are not rich in architectural inscriptions. True, one would not look for epigraphical display on the Gothic exteriors of the Madonna del Orto, of S. Zanipolo, of S. Maria Gloriosa dei Frari; nor would one expect to find a legible message from the architect where the great Byzantine basilica fringes the Piazza S. Marco with a palisade of domes and porches,[1] or where the church of the Salute assembles its cold and complicated beauties beside the waters of the Grand Canal. But the classic designs of Palladio afforded an opportunity of following the Roman practice, and two of his three Venetian church-fronts are inscribed. The Redentore (late 1570s) is bare of inscriptions, but S. Giorgio Maggiore (mid-1560s) carries, over its *portone*, a huge panel with a record in fine letters of the foundation and the completion of the church and, on either wing, under an urn surmounted by a memorial bust, a tribute to one of the two Doges who were the most conspicuous benefactors of the monastery. There is nothing remarkable about any of these texts, but the inscription on the central panel is impressive by virtue of its large scale and clear lettering; and, though none of the texts was composed until the façade was finally added to the building in 1610, it seems plain that the panel and the memorials, which would have been incomplete without inscriptions, must have formed part of the original design.

It is S. Francesco della Vigna, however, that provides the most elaborate example of Palladian epigraphy, and the case is so extraordinary that I make no excuse for going into it in detail.

The existing façade of S. Francesco was designed by Palladio in 1564; the church itself had been built from the designs of Sansovino thirty years before. Originally, as so often was the case, another church had stood upon the site;

[1] The domes and porches themselves carry a host of inscriptions in mosaic; but these are not elements in the architectural design.

41

but that fell into decay, and in 1534 the Patriarch of Aquileia, Giovanni Grimani, offered to build a new one, and chose Sansovino as architect. Criticism having been directed against Sansovino's designs, they were submitted by the Doge, Andrea Gritti, to the judgment of Francesco Giorgi, a Franciscan belonging to the monastery adjacent to the church. Giorgi produced a memorandum (dated 1 April 1535) analysing and approving (with some amendment) the architectural principles on which Sansovino's design was based, and this memorandum was itself submitted to three judges, Titian, Serlio, and Fortunio Spira, who countersigned it with their approval on 25 April 1535.[1]

When the first stone of the new church was laid on 15 August 1534,[2] two medals had been struck to commemorate the occasion, one by Andrea Spinelli, the other by Antonio Gambello or one of his pupils.[3] On the obverse of each of these medals is a bust of the Doge; on the reverse, the façade of the church. The representations of the façade shown on the medals bear little or no resemblance to the existing façade. How far either of them corresponds to Sansovino's original design one cannot tell, for, though his designs were approved and the new church rose on the site of its predecessor, the façade he had planned for it was never executed, because it did not please the Patriarch. For thirty years S. Francesco stood—again, like so many Venetian churches—with 'a base and brickish front', until, in 1564, Palladio produced a design that commended itself to the authorities, and that is the façade that we see today.[4]

The most striking thing about this façade is the profusion and prominence

[1] The text of this memorandum is printed by G. Moschini, *Guida per la Città di Venezia* (1815), I, i, 55–61; a translation is to be found in Prof. Wittkower's *Architectural Principles in the Age of Humanism* (1949), pp. 136–8.

[2] Correr, *Venezia e le sue lagune* (1847), II, part II, p. 231.

[3] G. F. Hill, *Corpus of Italian Medals of the Renaissance* (1930), reproduces a photograph representing a medal (no. 463), which he says 'has been attributed to Andrea Spinelli, but is not in his dry and wiry style; it is closer to Gambello, and possibly by him, but more probably by a pupil'. Temanza, in his Life of Sansovino (Venice, 1752, p. 18), prints an engraving of a medal, 'che in bronzo io conservo'. The reverse of it, he says, 'mostra la facciata sul campo, quale fu ideata da Jacopo'. One might have supposed that Temanza's medal was the same as that described by Hill, but the discrepancies between the pictures of the façade on the obverse seem too great; Temanza's clearly depicts a cupola absent from the other version, and he says expressly in his text that 'la cupola sopra la Tribuna', 'che non fu eseguita', was 'espressa nella medaglia'. Moreover, his medal (if his engraver is to be trusted) carried the date 1534 and was signed 'AN.SP.F', whereas Hill's medal is neither signed nor dated.

[4] It was slow in getting under way—when Vasari saw it in 1568 (T. Temanza, *Vita di Palladio*, 1762, page LII) 'era murato da pie tutto l'imbasamento'—and the statues were not executed (by Tiziano Aspetti) until about 1590.

of its inscriptions (Plate 16). These, and the device of the eagle in the pediment, and the two great statues—Moses, holding the Tables of the Law,
upon the spectator's left; St Paul, holding a book, upon his right—are more
than ornaments: they form an essential part of the design.[1] What do these
inscriptions mean? What, in particular, is the meaning of the key words
VTRIVSQVE TEMPLI in the main inscription?

To one who bears in mind the history of the two churches successively
built upon the site, the eagle, accompanied as it is by the word 'renovabitur',[2]
suggests an answer. The eagle, for Albertus Magnus and the natural historians
whose theories are preserved in mediaeval bestiaries and perpetuated by
Renaissance emblematists, stood for, among other things, *renovatio vitae*.

The two 'temples', then, are the original church and the new church, the
original church being 'renewed' in the substance of its successor. Of the two
churches, the long inscription may seem to tell us, God was the architect and
also the restorer.

Tempting though it is at first sight, this interpretation will not bear a closer
scrutiny: God might well, indeed, be called *aedificator* of both the churches, in
that he was responsible for the building of both of them: but, while he might
be said to have been *reparator* of the old church, in that he replaced it by the
new, of the new church he was *reparator* in no sense at all. Clearly we must look
elsewhere for an explanation.[3]

It is, I suggest, in the architectural principles underlying the design for the
building that we shall find the answer to our riddle.

[1] All the inscriptions (save RENOVABITVR, which is cut in the stone), and the two statues, are in bronze.
[2] Plainly a reference to Psalm cii. 5, in the Vulgate version: *Renovabitur sicut aquilae iuventus tua. Renovabitur
ut aquila* is an inscription on the tomb erected for the urn of Pope Nicholas IV in S. Maria Maggiore in
Rome by Cardinal Felice Peretti (afterwards Pope Sixtus V) in 1574: the designer of the monument was
Alessandro Cioli (see R. Lanciani, 'Il mausoleo di Nicolò IV', *Ausonia*, 1, Rome, 1906, pp. 96–9).
[3] A subtler interpretation of the phrase *utriusque templi* suggests itself if we consider the structural principles
on which Palladio's façade was designed. Professor Wittkower (*op. cit.* pp. 80–7) has analysed the
difficulty that faced architects who, like Palladio, wished to combine the classic temple-front and the
structure of a Christian basilica, with its nave and two aisles: a simple pedimented façade cannot, he
says, be made to cover, without grotesque enlargement or distortion, the breadth of the interior.

Wittkower explains at length how Palladio dealt with this problem in his three great Venetian church-
fronts—the Redentore, S. Giorgio Maggiore, and S. Francesco della Vigna. Briefly, his theory is that
Palladio's design is based on and embodies 'two interpenetrating temple fronts'. If this is a correct
analysis, Palladio's façade comprised—secretly, as it were—elements from two classical temples, and one
might be tempted to suggest that these are the 'two temples' that the inscription refers to. But here again
the explanation breaks down with the word *reparatori*, to which it gives no sense whatever in relation
to either *templum*.

16. Diagram of the façade of S. Francesco della Vigna, Venice (Palladio, 1564).

It was a commonplace of Renaissance architectural theory that the proportions of a building should correspond with, or be based on, those displayed in the human body. This was laid down by Vitruvius, who declared, 'Non potest aedes ulla sine symmetria atque proportione rationem habere compositionis, nisi uti ad hominis bene figurati membrorum habuerit exactam rationem.'[1] Having expounded the proportions that the various members bear to each other in a human body, and dilated upon the perfections therein displayed, Vitruvius proceeds: 'Ergo, si ita natura composuit corpus hominis uti proportionibus membra ad summam figurationem eius respondeant, cum causa constituisse videntur antiqui, ut etiam in operum perfectionibus singu-

[1] *De Architectura*, III, i.

44

lorum membrorum ad universam figurae speciem habeant commensus exactionem'—and this applies particularly, he says, to the temples of the Gods: 'Igitur, cum in omnibus operibus ordines traderent, id maxime in aedibus deorum, in quibus operum laudes et culpae aeternae solent permanere.'

This purely pagan theory was given a Biblical, and even a Christian, explanation by commentators in the many editions of Vitruvius that were published during the first half of the sixteenth century;[1] and of this explanation Palladio was well aware. In 1556, only half a dozen years before he designed the front of S. Francesco, Palladio supplied the illustrations to an edition of the *De Architectura* translated by his friend Daniele Barbaro, Patriarch of Aquileia.[2] Barbaro's comment on the opening of the passage quoted above from Vitruvius is as follows: 'La natura maestra ce insegna come havemo à reggersi nelle misure e nelle proportioni delle fabbriche à i Dei consecrate, imperoche non da altro ella vuole che impariamo le ragioni delle Simmetrie che ne i Tempi usar dovemo, che dal Sacro Tempio fatto ad imagine, e simiglianza di Dio, che è l'huomo.'

This religious justification of Vitruvius' aesthetic theory—that the human body was to be taken as a model in the construction of sacred buildings because it was itself a sacred Temple made after the likeness of the Deity—had already been adopted by Giorgi in his memorandum on the design for S. Francesco, and Sansovino made use of Vitruvius' principle in determining the proportions of the interior of the church. Wittkower concluded that the contents of Giorgi's memorandum were known also to Palladio, when, a generation later, he submitted his design for the façade.[3] The following passage from the memorandum surely puts it beyond doubt that Palladio was indeed familiar with it, and explains not only the architectural principles that guided him but also the inscriptions that form so conspicuous an element in his design: 'We, being desirous of building the church, have thought it necessary and most appropriate to follow that order of which God, the greatest architect, is the master and author. When God wished to instruct Moses concerning the form

[1] Wittkower (*op. cit.*) refers not only to the passage from Daniele Barbaro's commentary on Vitruvius quoted below, but also to the editions of Fra Giocondo (Venice, 1511) and Cesare Cesariano (Como, 1521), and to Giorgi's MS *Trattato di architectura*.

[2] It was for Daniele and his brother, Marc' Antonio, that Palladio built the Villa Maser, near Asolo.

[3] 'It appears certain that Palladio, when executing the façade of S. Francesco a generation later, knew Giorgi's memorandum and derived from it the mysterious 27 moduli which constituted the width of the central portion of his façade corresponding to the nave' (*op. cit.* p. 94).

and proportion of the tabernacle which he had to build, He gave him as model the fabric of the world, and said (as is written in Exodus, 25) "And look that thou make them after this pattern, which was showed thee in the Mount". By this pattern was meant, according to all the interpreters, the fabric of the world, and rightly so, because it was necessary that the particular place should resemble His universe, not in size, of which He has no need, nor in delight, but in proportion, which He wills should be not only in the material places, in which He dwells, but particularly in us, of whom Paul says, writing to the Corinthians, "Ye are the Temple of God".'[1]

The first, then, of the two temples referred to in the inscription is the church of S. Francesco itself, the temple made with hands; the second is the human body, the temple of the Holy Spirit. God was responsible for the building of the original church of S. Francesco and for its restoration in the shape of the new church; He is the architect also of the human body, and its 'restorer' in the 'new body' of the Resurrection, of which the eagle in the pediment is the symbol.

This explains not only the inscription but the choice of subjects for the bronze figures that fill the niches on the façade: it was to Moses that God revealed the proportions of the fabric of the world to be a pattern for his Tabernacle, the proportions of which corresponded with those of the human body; it was St Paul who called the body a Temple of the Holy Spirit. In making his statues of Moses and St Paul, Tiziano Aspetti must have been carrying out Palladio's directions, if not actually executing his original designs.[2]

The distinction between these two 'Temples' is maintained in the inscriptions on the lower ranges of the front: ACCEDE AD HOC—the summons to attend the place of worship—is placed over the head of Moses, builder of the Tabernacle; the injunction not to desert the spiritual Temple—NE DESERAS SPIRITVALE—is placed over the head of St Paul, who christened the body the Temple of the Holy Spirit.

A similar contrast shows itself in the pair of inscriptions on the lowest range: NON SINE IVGI EXTERIORI INTERIORIQUE BELLO: 'Not without an

---

[1] I quote Wittkower's translation, op. cit. p. 136. The most apposite Pauline reference is 1 Corinthians vi. 19: 'Know ye not that your body is the temple of the Holy Ghost which is in you?'

[2] In the notes added to the later editions of Francesco Sansovino's Venetia (I have used the edition of 1663), it is pointed out that the statue of Moses is inscribed at its foot Ministro Umbrarum, that of St Paul, Dispensatori Lucis. These inscriptions are barely legible today.

46

unceasing external and internal struggle'—the external struggle being allotted, as it were, to Moses upon the left, the internal struggle to St Paul upon the right.[1]

Palladio's attempt to express an intellectual conception by means of a united effort of the sculptural, the epigraphic, and the architectural arts is not very likely to succeed in its appeal to a twentieth-century observer. To an age that prefers to take its architecture neat, with no admixture of religious doctrine or of moral exhortation, an age lacking belief in the resurrection of the body, not easily impressed by mystical analogies, unaccustomed to being told to go to church, and none too sure about its Latin—to such an age the text-encumbered surface of S. Francesco may well present a jumble of ineffective incongruities. But to the eye of the Renaissance that surface must have seemed one complex whole, entirely harmonious and compellingly evocative. The great bronze letters—ACCEDE AD HOC—summoned the worshipper with a voice as clear and commanding as if it had sounded from a belfry; the twin statues— *Minister Umbrarum* and *Dispensator Lucis*—spoke reassuringly of the Old Dispensation and the New; the ascending eagle was an earnest of man's own corporeal resurrection; while the very proportions of the structure, seen in the light of the message that it carried on its face, exemplified the perfection of that human form which, sown in dishonour, would be raised a spiritual body.

[1] What is the meaning of this last series of words? Guide-books and historians (none of whom, by the way, has anything to say about the other inscriptions on the façade) can only suggest that it refers to disputes that beset the erection of the church. Domenico Martinelli, in *Il Ritratto di Venezia* (Venice, 1684), gives a full description of the façade, quoting all the inscriptions; but the only one he ventures to explain is RENOVABITVR—'alludendo', he says, 'alle parole della Sacra Scrittura: Renouabitur ut Aquila iuventus tua'.

I find in *Venetae Urbis Descriptio*, a poem in twelve Books written by Nicander Jasseus in 1760 and published in Venice in 1780, the following lines referring to S. Francesco della Vigna:

> Dum templo excedis, descriptum in fronte notabis
> Hanc quondam exortam magna inter jurgia molem—

to which is appended the note 'Inter varias templi inscriptiones en etiam est: Non sine iugi interiori exteriorique bello'.

Temanza (*Vita di Palladio*) describes at some length Palladio's work on this façade, adding: 'Comecche molte inscrizioni adornino questa egregia mole, quelle fra gli intercolonnii delle due Ale, per me si reputano da non passarsi sotto silenzio. Sulla destra vi si legge: *Non sine jugi interiori*, sulla sinistra *exteriorique bello*, che vengono interpretate alludere a disparere o discordia nata dell'erezione dell'opera stessa. Se poi tale discordia riguardasse l'Architetto, o l'Edificatore, se l'indovini chi puo.'

Moschini (*Guida, loc. cit.*), before giving the text of Giorgi's memorandum, quotes the text of this inscription, and observes, 'Se non vi ha di mistico, par che vi si alluda alle contese insorte sulle proporzioni fra procuratori interni ed esterni del chiostro.' Tassini (*Curiosità Veneziane*) suggests the same explanation.

47

The visible words of the architect at once adorned, explained, and animated his majestic composition.

THE INSCRIPTION IN PAINTING

If we find it difficult to accept from an architect a written text as an element in his work, we are scarcely happier when the same offer is made to us by a painter. If our eyes have been conditioned by non-representational painting, the 'significance' of which resides simply in the mysterious effectiveness of shapes and colours, and which does not ask us to understand or even to recognise its content, we have to make an uncomfortable adjustment if we are to enjoy a written text as an integral part of a picture. Even in a figurative composition, which contains recognisable features, shapes that represent or suggest natural objects or artefacts or living beings—things that lodge it, so to speak, in the realm of the articulate—a written text must seem to most spectators nowadays an alien and intrusive element.

In this respect European art presents a contrast to the art of the Far East, in which the image and the inscription go hand in hand, in an alliance made all the easier by the fact that Oriental script is itself pictorial while Oriental art is calligraphic.

The Renaissance spectator, however, evidently found no difficulty, whether he was confronted by a building or by a picture, in looking, as it were, with one eye while he read with the other, and the artists of the time ministered to that double vision. Inscriptions are strewn lavishly over the surfaces not only of buildings but of pictures in the Quattrocento and the Cinquencento, and these picture-inscriptions are of very many kinds. The script may be Roman or Gothic; the letters may be capital or cursive; the words may be represented as cut with a chisel or written with a brush or pen; the language may be Latin or vernacular; the text may be religious or secular, its form may be verse or prose, and its source may be either a quotation (i.e. a Biblical, classical, or modern phrase or passage, or a proverb or motto) or an original composition (i.e. something written specially in order to be included in the picture). Further, the inscription may be an integral part of the scene represented or it may be imposed upon that scene *ab extra*; it may serve as a label or act as a message; and, in using script as a part of his pictorial apparatus, the artist may

48

be following a tradition that is ecclesiastical or classical or, in a loose sense, heraldic.

Very interesting inquiries that take as their starting-point the physical attributes of picture-inscriptions have been pursued by Professor Millard Meiss[1] and Dr Dario Covi;[2] less attention, I think, has been paid to the evidential value of their texts. Those who are interested in picture-inscriptions because they show how ubiquitous the epigraph became in the artistic consciousness of the Renaissance will be concerned rather to ascertain the intentions of the painter. When he incorporated a written text in his work, how, they will ask, did he fit it into the scheme of his picture, and what part did he intend it to play in the total effect produced? And how far was he successful in his aim? Of course the answers to these questions vary from one artist, and one picture, to another.

Sometimes the inscription is 'internal'—that is, it is an integral part of the scene depicted, or belongs more or less closely to that scene; sometimes it is, as it were, imposed upon it.[3] The distinction must not be pressed too hard, for it is not always possible to say that a representational artist is 'depicting' a 'scene', or to say what is meant by describing something as belonging to the scene depicted and something else as belonging to the world of reality. Such phrases conceal fundamental problems about the meaning of 'representation' in art and about the degrees of 'reality' that individual artists, so far as they were conscious of the problem, would have recognised as being reflected in their creations. These are perplexing questions, and I should soon be out of my depth, both in aesthetics and in the history of art, if I attempted to explore them.

Sometimes, however, there is no difficulty in supporting the distinction between an 'internal' and an 'imposed' inscription, corresponding to the

[1] In his book *Andrea Mantegna as Illuminator* (New York, 1957) and his article 'Toward a more comprehensive Renaissance Palaeography', *The Art Bulletin*, XLII (1960), 97-112.

[2] In his article 'Lettering in Fifteenth Century Florentine Painting', *The Art Bulletin*, XLV (1963), 1-17. I have not seen Dr Covi's unpublished dissertation *The Inscription in Fifteenth Century Florentine Painting*, presented in 1958 at the Institute of Fine Arts in New York University.

[3] In a non-representational painting there is no place for an inscription of either of these kinds, for there is no depicted scene in which an inscription can be incorporated or on which it can be imposed. The non-representational painter, however, can incorporate an inscription in his work in another way, viz. literally, by making it—as where a piece of a newspaper forms part of a *collage*—a bodily part of his composition.

distinction between a world re-created by the artist and the 'real' world in which he actually lives. In many pictures of the Crucifixion, for instance, two scrolls of paper or parchment (*cartellini*) are attached to the Cross, one at the top, the other at the foot; the first bearing the letters INRI, the second, the signature of the painter. Of such a pair of inscriptions the first must be called 'internal', the second, 'imposed'. Neither is a very significant example of its kind, for the INRI *cartellino* is an almost inevitable feature of the Crucifixion scene,[1] while the artist's signature contributes no more to the asethetic effect of the picture than if it had simply been affixed to its frame.[2]

More fruitful than the distinction between 'internal' and 'imposed' inscriptions, though ultimately no less evanescent, is the distinction between inscriptions that are merely descriptive labels and those that are intended to suggest—to carry a message, as it were, from the artist to the spectator.

The most familiar type of 'label' in Renaissance painting is the holy name or brief text that appears so often in religious pictures—the title spelt out round the martyr's halo; the parchment unfurled by a prophet or held aloft by an attendant angel; the page of Holy Writ over which the hermit or the saint is poring; the mystic words—ECCE AGNUS DEI: AVE MARIA GRATIAE PLENA—hovering above the heads of sacred persons, or inscribed upon a scroll that seems to issue from their mouths. Usually the text, if it is not simply a name, consists of a familiar phrase or phrases, and serves only to identify or attach a label to a figure or an occasion. Sometimes, however, the label, in the very act of identifying, may intensify for the spectator echoes and associa-

[1] But even the familiar INRI *cartellino* may be so introduced as to obtain an unexpected emotional effect. Recently a little picture ascribed to Hans Holbein the elder was put up for sale at Sotheby's (2 July 1965, Lot 8, 'The Property of a Nobleman'); it represents a coarse-looking fellow, in workman's dress of the painter's own day, seated on a bench facing the spectator, busy writing on a scroll that he holds upon his knee. A large bone-handled gimlet is stuck into the plank beside him; at his right hand is an ink-pot, in his left he holds a bag of sand. At a first glance, the picture appears to represent a homely scene with no remarkable feature, and the journeyman seems to be intent upon a task of no especial significance; on a closer look, one recognises with a peculiar thrill the letters he is writing and the purpose that his scroll will shortly have to serve.

[2] The painter's signature, though sometimes cunningly incorporated (e.g. as the signature of a letter), is usually as 'external' to the composition as if it had been affixed to the frame. But sometimes the frame and an inscription upon it (e.g. Bedoli's *La Concezione* in the gallery at Parma) seem to have been specially designed to be a part, as it were, of the picture. Who is to say where a picture begins and where it ends? And what is the relation between a picture and its title? And what of the poetical extracts (from his fictitious *Fallacies of Time*) that Turner appended to the titles of his pictures in exhibition catalogues—were they not intended to play a part in the total effect produced by the picture?

tions already evoked by the representation; the label may connote, as a logician might put it, as well as denote, like the name upon a monument commemorating a great figure or a historic event.

Innumerable pictures might be chosen to exemplify the distinction between the inscription that is merely a label, and the inscription that is a label but at the same time something more. We will take a pair of Florentine frescoes, both representing the Last Supper: one, in S. Apollonia, by Andrea del Castagno; the other, now in the Museo di S. Marco, by Domenico Ghirlandaio (Plates 17, 18).

In Castagno's picture, the inscriptions on the floor-ledge are mere labels, identifying the Apostles; they add nothing to the composition or to its impact on the emotions of the spectator.[1] In Ghirlandaio's presentation of the scene, the inscription (taken *verbatim* from the Vulgate version of Luke xxii. 29–30: *Ego dispono vobis sicut disposuit mihi Pater meus regnum ut edatis et bibatis super mensam meam in regno meo*) serves a double purpose: as pure ornament, it enlivens the frieze that runs from one extremity of the picture to the other; at the same time, for those who understand the text, it binds the company together round their central figure—with EGO and MEO at either end and REGNUM set firmly over the Saviour's head—and, while it may be said to be in a sense a label, descriptive of the scene, it endows that scene, for those who reflect upon its significance, with an added spiritual dimension.

Professor Meiss has called attention in a recent article[2] to two Quattrocento pictures representing the infant Jesus asleep in his Mother's arms, each of which contains an inscription that is a label and at the same time something more. In one, by Neri di Bicci (present whereabouts unknown), the Child holds a scroll on which is written a quotation from the Song of Solomon: EGHO DORMIVI ET CHOR MEVM VIGILAT; in the other, by Cosimo Tura (in the Accademia, Venice), a ledge at the foot of the picture is

[1] In his fresco of the Last Supper in the Monastero di Foligno in Florence (1485–93) Perugino employs exactly the same device of labelling the Apostles on the floor-ledge. When the fresco was uncovered in 1845 it was attributed to Raphael, partly because it was thought possible to spell out of the gold *ghirigori* that decorated the border of the tunic of St Thomas the date MDV and the letters RAP VR (see F. Canuti, *Il Perugino*, Siena, 1931, I, 69, n. 2).

[2] 'Sleep in Venice, Ancient Myths and Renaissance Proclivities', *Proceedings of the American Philosophical Society*, vol. 110, no. 5, October 1966, pp. 348–82. Professor Meiss reproduces the Nero di Bicci and the Tura, and alludes in a footnote to another such inscribed picture, a Madonna in the Correr in Venice, signed by Jacobello del Fiore, which carries the legend IN GREMIO MATRIS SEDE SAPIENTIAE—evidently an allusion to the identification of the Virgin with the seat of Divine Wisdom.

17. Andrea del Castagno, *Last Supper*: Florence, Museo del Castagno.

Detail from plate 17

18. Domenico Ghirlandaio, *Last Supper*: Florence, Convento di S. Marco.

inscribed SVIGLIA EL TUO FILIO DOLCE MADRE PIA PER FAR INFIN FELICE LALMA MIA.

The first of these inscriptions is internal: the words are the imagined utterance of the Child; the second external: the prayer it contains is the spectator's. Each directs our attention, as Professor Meiss points out, to a spiritual meaning latent in the scene; the first reminds us that Christ, even as a sleeping infant, is the shepherd of our souls; the second calls upon the Mother to wake the Child so that he may continue the work of redemption. In each case, one may say that the effect produced upon the spectator by the picture would be different if he were unaware of the inscription, or did not know what it meant.

A more sophisticated use of an inscription that seems at first sight to serve the purpose only of a label was made by Botticelli in one of the most famous of his pictures, the *Madonna of the Magnificat* in the Uffizi. Walter Pater, in his essay on Botticelli, describes the Child in this picture as guiding his Mother's hand 'to transcribe in a book the words of her exaltation, the *Ave* and the *Magnificat*, and the *Gaude Maria*, and the young angels,' he says, 'glad to rouse her for a moment from her dejection, are eager to hold the ink-horn and to support the book; but the pen almost drops from her hand, and the high cold words have no meaning for her'. As so often, Pater's iconography is at fault but his critical instinct is sound: the 'high cold words', plainly legible in the book in which the Virgin has been writing, are indeed the words of the *Magnificat*; but the Child is not, as Pater supposed, guiding his mother's hand to write 'the words of her exaltation'; he is touching with his finger a word she has already written. That word is *humilitatem*—'the lowliness of thy handmaiden' (Plate 19).[1]

A book displaying the text of the *Magnificat* is a traditional 'property' in pictures of the Virgin and Child or the Annunciation—a 'label' almost as familiar as the 'INRI' *cartellino* in pictures of the Crucifixion. But here Botticelli has made it something more.

The humility of the Madonna—combined by a mystical paradox with her exaltation—provided a theme, and a title, for a phase in her iconography that 'attained a vast popularity in the late fourteenth and early fifteenth centuries

[1] This was pointed out to me by Professor Edgar Wind.

53

19. Botticelli, *Madonna of the Magnificat*: Florence, Uffizi.

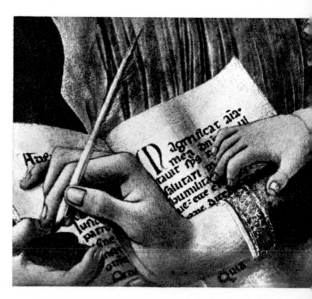

Detail from plate 19

in Italy, and appeared, beyond Italy, in Spain, France, and Germany'.[1] That phase, the Madonna of Humility, according to Professor Meiss, is 'really identified, in a sense, with one period, the Trecento and early Quattrocento'; its title has reference to the Madonna's lowly seat upon the ground.[2] Botticelli, more sophisticated than his predecessors, chose to express the Virgin's humility as a psychological rather than a physical phenomenon.

No critic has attempted to catalogue the postures in which the infant Christ was represented in painting and in sculpture in the Quattrocento.[3] The painters of the preceding century rarely, it seems, depict the Child as reading; but sometimes he glances 'at the book held by the Virgin and points to the words (*which vary in each case* [my italics]) with his right forefinger'.[4]

I do not know how painters of the Quattrocento most often portrayed the Child in relation to the book, but it was not by chance that in the *Madonna of the Magnificat* Botticelli represented him as indicating the word *humilitatem*. At all events it is certain that the painter was deliberate in his choice of the moment at which the Child is shown as making this gesture: it is the moment when the Madonna has written the word *Quia*—the first word of the sentence *Quia fecit mihi magna qui potens est:* 'For he that is mighty hath magnified me.' It is just as she has reached 'the words of her exaltation' that he checks her with his thumb upon her wrist, and with his finger indicates the word 'humility'.

At first sight, it might seem that it cannot be *this* 'Quia' that the Madonna has just transcribed, for the following reason: her forearm lies across the page on which she has been writing, hiding half a dozen lines of the text; *humilitatem* appears above her wrist, *Quia* below it; now, in the text of the *Magnificat*, the sentence *Quia fecit mihi magna* is separated by only a dozen words from the word *humilitatem*; the Virgin must therefore have transcribed that sentence already, in the first (or the first and second) of the lines hidden by her arm, and the *Quia* that appears below her wrist, six lines lower down, must (it might be argued) be a *Quia* occurring later in the text. But there is in fact no later instance of *Quia* (or, indeed, of *quia*) in the text of the *Magnificat*.

[1] See Professor Millard Meiss's learned and exhaustive article in *The Art Bulletin*, XVIII (1936), 435–64.
[2] It does not appear, in any of the examples given by Professor Meiss, to be iconographically connected with the words of the Magnificat (though the relevant passage in St Luke is alluded to in an inscription upon one of the pictures he refers to—*op. cit.* p. 435, n. 2), and indeed a book would be quite out of place in most if not all of the types of the Madonna of Humility that he distinguishes.
[3] As Mrs Dorothy Shorr has done for the Trecento: *The Christ Child in Devotional Images during the XIV Century* (New York, 1954).   [4] Shorr, *op. cit.* p. 191.

It is plain, therefore, not only that it is this phrase, *Quia fecit mihi magna*, that Botticelli intended to indicate by his *Quia*, but also that he has deliberately postponed the word by several lines[1]—and why, if not in order to reveal it, below the Mother's wrist, as the point in her writing at which she is interrupted by the gesture of the Child?

If it is said that this is to read too much into what must be the chance gesture of an as yet unlettered infant, the objection can be answered from a relevant contemporary document; indeed, to suggest that the Child could not read what his mother was writing would have been positively heretical. Antonino, Archbishop of Florence, in his *Summa Theologica* (*c.* 1450), gives a list of the ways in which painters may offend the pious: 'Reprehensibiles etiam sunt', he says, 'cum pingunt ea, quae sunt contra fidem', and he includes among his examples of such heretical imagery, 'cum faciunt…parvulum Jesum cum tabula litterarum, quum non didicerit ab homine'[2]—the Child needed no human spelling-master, he knew from birth, by divine instinct, how to read.

It is not, then, by chance that, as the angels hold the crown above his Mother's head, and as she herself is about to transcribe the words of her exaltation, the Child, by a private, and almost secret, gesture, draws her attention (and the spectator's) to her 'lowliness': Botticelli, by means of the

[1] Botticelli might have been expected to represent the Virgin either as continuing the text at the point she would have reached had the space hidden by her wrist and sleeve been filled with writing, or, less realistically, as resuming it from the point at which it begins to be hidden. He did neither, but made her resume it at an intermediate point which, unless the suggestion I have made in the text is accepted, must have been quite arbitrarily chosen.

[2] I owe my knowledge of this passage to Mr Creighton Gilbert's article 'The Archbishop on the Painters of Florence, 1450', *The Art Bulletin*, XLI (1959), 75–87. Mr Gilbert and I, however, take the Archbishop's condemnation in opposite senses. Mr Gilbert thinks that Antonino is condemning artists who represent the Child as reading in a book at an age when he must have been still unlettered—'when he had not learned from man' in his translation of *quum non didicerit ab homine*. I, on the other hand, think that Antonino is condemning those who represent the Child with a spelling-tablet although he did not learn his letters from a human teacher. Mr Gilbert's view involves taking *quum* with the subjunctive as 'when' and *didicerit* as a pluperfect; it gives no point to *ab homine*, and it makes *cum tabula litterarum* (which he indeed translates simply by 'with a tablet of letters') necessarily imply ability to read. It is plain that Mr Gilbert's interpretation is what I represent it to be, for he accepts the alternative reading *ab nomine* (from an eighteenth-century edition of Antonino's *Summa*) as possible Latin, thinks that 'when he had not yet learned beyond his name' is an acceptable (though 'rather forced') translation of it, and adds, 'Fortunately this does not seem to alter Antonino's argument at all.'

But even if Mr Gilbert's translation were acceptable, the sense he gives to the words would not fit in, as mine does, with Antonino's context: to represent the Child with a spelling-tablet plainly suggests that he was dependent upon human teachers, which would certainly be, as Antonino says, *contra fidem*; but there would surely be nothing heretical in the suggestion that he was a preternaturally precocious reader.

text that he has made a part of his picture, has given us a Quattrocento version, more sophisticated and literary than the Trecento's, of the Madonna of Humility.

Was it like Botticelli thus to convey a secret message to the spectator by means of a quotation? This is just what he does, albeit in a rather different way, in another picture of the Virgin.

The inscribed book in the *Madonna of the Magnificat* is an integral part of the depicted scene; the inscription is 'internal' to the picture. In the altar-piece that he painted for the church of S. Barnaba in Florence, Botticelli conveyed a message by means of an inscription of a quite different kind—an 'imposed' inscription that forms no part of the representation and is not supposed to be present to the consciousness of the persons represented: cut in the marble steps of the throne on which the Virgin is standing, hardly to be perceived except by one who looks intently for it, is the line with which Dante invokes her in the last Canto of the *Paradiso*:

Vergine Madre, figlia del tuo figlio.[1]

Botticelli, said Pater, 'is before all things a poetical painter, blending the charm of story and sentiment, the idiom of the art of poetry, with the charm of line and colour, the medium of abstract painting'. He was, of course, a student of Dante; he illustrated the *Divina Commedia* and is said to have written a commentary upon it. Whether or not we take this visual quotation of an actual line from the poem as a practical illustration of Botticelli's tendency to 'poeticise' his pictures, it is certainly an instance, like the *Madonna of the Magnificat*, of his conveying in paint a written message to the spectator.

Botticelli was not the only artist of the time to commit to paint that message from the *Divina Commedia*. In the Museum of Leghorn there is a Madonna by an anonymous painter[2] which contains not merely the first line, but nine lines—the first three stanzas—of Dante's celebrated invocation. The verses are embroidered on the hem of the Virgin's robe, in characters so small and intricately woven that it is hardly possible to read them.

[1] *Paradiso*, XXXIII, 1; the next line, 'Umile ed alta più che creatura', describes the same union of humility and exaltation that the painter expressed in the *Madonna of the Magnificat*.

[2] See Mario Salmi, 'La Madonna "Dantesca" del Museo di Livorno e il "Maestro della Natività di Castello"', *Liburni Civitas*, LII (1938), Fasc. V–VI, pp. 5–44. I am indebted to Mr Everett Fahy for drawing my attention to the existence of this picture.

QVI COELVM CECINIT MEDIVMQVE IMVMQVE TRIBVNAL   LVSTRAVITQVE ANIMO CVNCTA POETA SVO   DOCTVS ADEST DANTES SVA QVEM FLORENTIA SAEPE
SENSIT CONSILIIS AC PIETATE PATRE   NIL POTVIT TANTO MORS SAEVA NOCERE POETAE   QVEM VIVVM VIRTVS CARMEN IMAGO FACIT

20. Domenico di Michelino, *Dante and Illustrations of the Divina Commedia*: Florence, Duomo.

Extreme examples like the *Madonna Dantesca* prompt one to ask the general question: how did artists intend such visual quotations to be taken by the spectator? It depends, we must answer, upon what kind of picture they appear in. An unsophisticated artist will label figures with their names simply because that is the clearest way of showing who they are meant to be—this was often done, for instance, by the painters of Greek vases. So, also, the writing embroidered on the Bayeux tapestry enabled those who could read it to follow, and to explain to others, the story told by the pictures; and the texts scattered so freely over the frescoes and mosaics in Byzantine churches helped the literate worshipper in his devotions, while they impressed the illiterate—like the liturgy sung in a language that he could not understand—with a sense of mystery and awe. When a Renaissance artist incorporated what I have

58

called 'label' inscriptions into religious pictures, he was no doubt influenced by this devotional tradition, and if his picture was a church fresco or an altar-piece, he was actually contributing to it.

When he was working for a private patron, however, the artist might be exposed to more sophisticated influences, and such freaks as the *Madonna Dantesca* are no doubt due to the whim of the person for whom the picture was painted.

An instructive contrast between the conventional 'label' and the 'literary' inscription with a special purpose may be seen in two other Dante pictures—the fresco by Domenico di Michelino in the Duomo of Florence, which shows the poet standing outside the city walls with the Mount of Purgatory in the background (Plate 20), and a sixteenth-century picture from the Kress collection, now in the National Gallery in Washington, in which Dante is seated,

21. Florentine School, *Allegorical Portrait of Dante*: Washington, D.C., National Gallery of Art (Samuel H. Kress Collection).

looking towards the Mount, with the Duomo in the distance behind him (Plate 21). In each picture the poet holds an open book; in Michelino's fresco the first lines of the *Commedia*, inscribed upon its pages, serve simply as a label indicating its contents; in the more sophisticated picture the pages display sixteen whole stanzas, written in a careful and legible script; they are the opening stanzas of Canto XXV of the *Paradiso* ('Se mai continga . . .'), and that passage was surely chosen by the patron who commissioned the picture in order to remind the spectator of Dante's feeling for his native city: it expresses and, for the spectator, intensifies the emotion that the painter has put into the poet's face.

Before the middle of the fifteenth century, there began to appear in Italian pictures inscriptions that owed nothing to any ecclesiastical or devotional tradition—inscriptions, usually painted to look as if they had been cut in stone, that imitated, or were derived from, classical Roman epigraphy.

Often, with Roman epigraphs in mind, a painter would inscribe his own name, or a name or motto identifying the subject of a portrait, on a stone parapet in front of the picture or on the surface of a marble object forming part of the composition.

One might expect inscriptions of this kind to be more frequent in Italy, where Roman remains were more abundant and classical influence was more immediate, than north of the Alps; and one might expect the texts to be in Latin (in so far as they comprised anything more than a proper name) and to be shown as being cut in Roman capitals. On the whole, it seems that these expectations are borne out by the evidence, and it is an odd anomaly that in two of the earliest pictures with stone parapets the inscriptions should be in the vernacular, and that one of them should be the work of a Northern artist.

The earliest example, it seems, of a parapet in Italian portraiture is the *Head of a Young Man*, ascribed to Uccello, in the Musée Benoît-Molin at Chambéry: it bears the motto EL FIN FA TUTTO. The other example is better known: it is Jan Van Eyck's portrait of a young man in the National Gallery, dated 1432; here again the inscription, which is carved in fanciful quasi-classical capitals, is in the vernacular. 'The figure', says Panofsky, 'emerges from behind a parapet on which the words LEAL SOVVENIR appear to have been engraved with a chisel, precisely as do the effigies of Roman soldiers or provincial artisans from their memorial tablets; and the chips and cracks in the stone of this parapet, indicative of venerable age, make the painter's archaeological intention even more obvious.'[1]

No Italian painter was a more passionate archaeologist than Mantegna,[2] and none was more deeply fascinated by the vision of classical Rome. That passion and that influence permeate his pictures and make themselves felt in the care he takes to reproduce accurately the dresses and accessories of the figures in his historical and allegorical compositions, and in the architectural settings and decorative motifs with which he adorns classical and non-classical subjects alike. He re-creates the Roman scene with the diligence and detailed accuracy of a classical scholar. It is no surprise to find in his *Triumph of Caesar* at Hampton Court, beside his mysterious 'pictographs',[3] accurate representations of Roman triumphal banners and standards with appropriate inscriptions.

Mantegna also introduced reproductions of actual Roman epigraphical remains into the frescoes with which in the 1450s he adorned the walls of the Ovetari Chapel in the Church of the Eremitani at Padua.

In *The Martyrdom of St Christopher* he reproduces, on a wall in the background, an inscription printed by Mommsen[4] from a copy among the papers of Furlanetto, an archaeologist of the early nineteenth century. The original stone has not survived; it was evidently mutilated before Furlanetto made his transcript, and Mantegna's picture is the sole authority for its last two lines.

Another inscription of which the original is now lost appears in the fresco representing *St James before Herod Agrippa*. Here again the text is recorded by Furlanetto and Mommsen;[5] it was also copied by Jacopo Bellini into a sketch-book now in the Louvre; Mantegna may have derived his text from Bellini's transcript or from the Roman original.

---

[1] 'Who is Jan Van Eyck's "Tymotheos"?', *The Journal of the Warburg and Courtauld Institutes*, XII (1949), p. 80—an article in which the author, with extreme but unconvincing ingenuity, argues that an 'imposed' inscription, lightly scrawled in Greek characters on the parapet above the deeply and realistically incised 'internal' motto, identifies the subject as a contemporary musician.

[2] One may recall the well-known account of his archaeological expedition on the Lago di Garda in 1464, together with Samuele da Tradate, Feliciano, and another (perhaps Marcanova), printed in full by Paul Kristeller in his *Mantegna* (1901), pp. 472–3. Feliciano indulges in a 'Jubilatio' over the 'magna antiquitatum mirabilia' discovered by the party.

[3] See Karl Giehlow, 'Die Hieroglyphenkunde des Humanismus in der Allegorie der Renaissance', *Jahrbuch des Kunsthistorischen Sammlungen in Wien*, XXXII (1915), 88–93.

[4] *C.I.L.* V, part I, no. 2989; see A. Moschetti, 'Le iscrizioni lapidarie romane negli affreschi del Mantegna agli Eremitani', *Atti del Istituto Veneto di Scienze, Lettere, ed Arti*, LXXXIX (1929–30), part II, pp. 227ff.

[5] *C.I.L.* V, part I, no. 2528; see Moschetti, *op. cit.*

Yet another inscription appears in the fresco *St James led to Execution* (Plate 22); the architectural background contains a medallion inscribed thus:

L VITRVVIVS CERDO ARCHITETVS

—which reproduces, either directly or from a contemporary transcript, the text of an inscription[1] on the (since dismantled) Arco dei Gavi at Verona.[2]

In all these three Ovetari frescoes, the inscriptions form an integral part of the scene depicted by the artist; they are mere copies, more or less faithful, of Roman originals; their texts are irrelevant to the subject-matter of the pictures and carry no special message to the spectator; it was enough for Mantegna that they were classical inscriptions, certifying the architecture (as it were) to be Roman, and thus adding vividly to the verisimilitude of his representation.

Into a contemporary copy of one of these pictures a message has been introduced, by substituting a vernacular motto for the classical original. The fresco is *St James led to Execution*; the copy, which is in the Musée Jacquemart-André in Paris and has been attributed to Francesco Benaglio (Plate 23),[3] while it reproduces the original faithfully in almost every other particular,[4] substitutes for the text in the medallion a motto presumably chosen by the painter:

LA VITA EL FIN

—an 'imposed' has been substituted for an 'internal' inscription; the Latin label has become a message in the vernacular.[5]

By the end of the fifteenth century, the quasi-classical epigraph, inscribed on a parapet or an object in the picture, had become a familiar feature, serving a variety of purposes, in Italian painting. With the turn of the century it became an increasingly common practice for painters to identify the subjects

---

[1] *C.I.L.* V, part I, no. 3464.

[2] For a very full discussion of the palaeographical aspect of these inscriptions, their derivation, and their relation to other inscriptions in Mantegna's pictures, see Professor Millard Meiss's article already referred to—'Toward a more comprehensive Renaissance Palaeography', *The Art Bulletin*, XLII (1960), 97–112.

[3] Who, according to the notice in Thieme-Becker, worked principally at Verona in the third quarter of the century.

[4] See Paul Mantz, *Gazette des Beaux-Arts*, XXXIII (1886), 183.

[5] The interpretation of this message remains a puzzle. Its resemblance to the vernacular motto on the parapet in the putative Uccello at Chambéry (see above) is presumably a coincidence. Giehlow (*loc. cit.*) suggests, unconvincingly, that the words were introduced in explanation of symbols appearing in the surrounding relief.

22. Mantegna, *St James led to Execution*: Padua, Church of the Eremitani.
(for detail see page 64)

23. *St James led to Execution*, old copy of Mantegna's fresco: Paris, Musée Jacquemart-André.

Detail from plate 22

Detail from plate 23

of their portraits by means of a motto, often accompanied by an emblem. This symbolic or emblematic use of the picture-inscription is quite distinct from the ecclesiastical and classical uses already described; it appealed to an age that enjoyed playing games with words and images and made a cult of the *impresa*.

Two Medici pictures now in the Uffizi illustrate very well how this fashion affected the art of portraiture.

The first is Pontormo's picture of Cosimo de' Medici 'il Vecchio', 'one of the great imaginative creations of Florentine portraiture' (Plate 24).[1] On the throne on which Cosimo is seated are inscribed, classically abbreviated, the words that the Florentines ordered to be engraved upon his tomb: COSMVS MEDICES PATER PATRIAE. Beside him springs a laurel tree with two branches; one has been broken off short; among the leaves of the other is twined a scroll bearing letters out of which it is possible, with difficulty, to spell the Virgilian quotation

VNO AVVLSO NON DEFICIT ALTER

The first of these inscriptions is no more than a label presenting Cosimo's Roman title in an appropriately classical epigraphic form; the second is a motto forming part of an *impresa*, and belongs to the Cinquecento picture rather than to its Quattrocento subject. Evidently the laurel, with its two branches, symbolises the *stirps Medicea*;[2] the quotation must surely signify the substitution of one ruler of that line for another. To what occasion does it refer?

A very plausible answer is suggested by Paolo Giovio's posthumously published *Dialogo dell' imprese militari e amorose*.[3] Speaking of the *imprese* of the Grand Duke Cosimo, who succeeded Alessandro de' Medici as ruler of Florence in 1537, Giovio says:

'Hebbene un'altra nel principio del suo principato, dottamente trouata dal Reuerendo M. Pier Francesco de' Ricci, suo Maiordomo; e fù quel che dice Vergilio nel VI del Eneida dal ramo d'oro col motto VNO AVVLSO NON DEFICIT ALTER, figurando un ramo suelto dell'albero, in luogo del quale ne succede subito un'altro; uolendo intendere, che se bene era stata leuata la uita

---

[1] See F. M. Clapp, *Jacopo Carucci da Pontormo, His Life and Work* (New Haven, 1916), pp. 147–52.

[2] One may recall Politian's dirge on the death of Lorenzo il Magnifico in 1492: *Laurus impete fulminis Illa, illa iacet subito*—though there the laurel no doubt refers also to the name Lorenzo (*impete* is Professor Eduard Fraenkel's suggestion for *impetu*—see 'Latin Verse of the High Renaissance', *Italian Renaissance Studies*, ed. E. F. Jacob, 1960, pp. 404–5, where the poem is quoted in full).

[3] First published in Rome in 1555.

24. Pontormo, *Cosimo de' Medici Pater Patriae*: Florence, Uffizi.

al Duca Alessandro, non mancaua un altro ramo d'oro nella medesima stirpe.'

The inscription on the scroll, it seems, was imported into the portrait of the Grand Duke's illustrious forebear in order to announce that a new Cosimo had appeared in the succession of the Medici, to take the place of the murdered Alessandro and revive the glories of his namesake.[1]

My second example of a portrait carrying an 'emblematic' inscription is a picture that hangs in the Uffizi close to Pontormo's Cosimo: Vasari's imaginary portrait of Lorenzo il Magnifico (Plate 25). Here also, inscriptions are associated with the representation of symbolic objects: the painter has presented Lorenzo seated with his face in profile looking to the spectator's right;[2] on his left hand, standing on a marble plinth, is a bronze *vas ansatum*, with a grotesque mask hanging from its long curved spout and another mask of hideous aspect lying upturned beside it on the plinth.

What is the meaning of the vase that plays so prominent a part in this composition? Those familiar with the Renaissance passion for the *impresa*, the *emblema*, and the *rebus*, may have little doubt about the answer: the vase is a cryptic signature of *Vasari*, whose family, by his own account,[3] took their name from an ancestor who was an expert potter—*vasaio* or *vasaro*.

One cannot say positively that this interpretation must be wrong, but it provides an insufficient explanation of the symbol, for it disregards the inscriptions that accompany it.

Lorenzo's right arm rests on a marble slab on which, incised in rough Roman

[1] According to Vasari (*Vite*, ed. Milanesi, VI, 1881, 264) this picture was painted for Goro Gheri when he was secretary to Lorenzo, Duke of Urbino, who died in 1519. It has accordingly been attributed by critics to a date some twenty years earlier than that which I suggest: Clapp (*Jacopo Carucci*, 1916), 1518–19; Toesca (*Il Pontormo*, 1943), *c.* 1523; Becherucci (*Manieristi Toscani*, 1944), 1518; Freedberg (*Painting of the High Renaissance*, 1961), 1518; Rearick (*Drawings of Pontormo*, 1964), 1518–19; Berti (*Pontormo*, 1964), 1518–20; Forster (*Pontormo*, 1966), 1518–19. I saw no ground for challenging the accepted dating when I delivered the Sandars Lectures in 1964, and could suggest no satisfactory application for the motto. Then Professor Edgar Wind drew my attention to the passage of Giovio quoted in the text, and pointed out to me its significance for the dating of the picture. Dr Price Zimmermann of Reed College, Portland, Oregon, supplied me with further evidence favouring the later date, which he found in a copy in the Riccardiana of the rare *Apparato e feste* celebrating Cosimo I's marriage in 1539, when one of the decorations of the *festa* consisted of a medallion containing the motto and *impresa* that appear in Pontormo's picture.

I have argued the case for the later date in an article, 'Pontormo's *Cosimo il Vecchio* A New Dating' in the *Journal of the Warburg and Courtauld Institutes*, XXX (November 1967), 163–75.

[2] Vasari reproduces this figure of Lorenzo very closely in the picture painted many years later, now in the Palazzo Vecchio, representing il Magnifico receiving presents brought by the ambassadors of the Sultan.

[3] See Vasari, *Vite*, ed. Milanesi (Florence, 1878), II, 553–61.

capitals, is the text SICVT MAIORES MIHI ITA ET EGO POSTERIS MEA VIRTVTE PRELVXI. On his left the theme of virtue is repeated: along the spout of the bronze vessel are inscribed the words PREMIVM VIRTVTIS, and on its body VIRTVTVM OMNIVM VAS, while the marble plinth that supports it carries, in capitals larger and clearer than the rest, the legend VITIA VIRTVTI SVBIACENT.

It is tempting to read into this complex of words and images both a general and a particular psychological truth: Vice, the artist seems to tell us, underlies Virtue and even supports it, for there is no virtue that has not its foundation in a nature in which vice and virtue are inextricably intertwined, and it is often from our vices that our virtues draw their strength—a Machiavellian observation that applies with especial aptness to Lorenzo, whose shrewd duplicity is written clearly on his face.

Unfortunately, evidence exists that proves this interpretation to be over-subtle. There is a letter written by Vasari to Alessandro de' Medici, who had commissioned the picture, in 1533 or 1534,[1] in which he outlines his programme for it, describing its principal features and setting out three of the inscriptions. True, Vasari does not mention 'Vitia Virtuti subiacent', but the following passage from his letter makes it plain what those words were intended to signify: 'Ho fatto', he says, 'una maschera brutissima, figurata per il Vitio, la quale stando a diacere in su la fronte, sara conculcata da un purissimo vaso, pien di rose et di viole, con queste lettere: Virtus[2] omnium vas.' The hideous mask, then, represents Vice, and 'conculcata' shows plainly that 'subiacent' must be read as if it were 'subiciuntur' or 'subiecta sunt': the picture is simply repeating, in words and images, the dubious commonplace that Virtue subdues and triumphs over Vice.

The inscriptions in Vasari's portrait, like VNO AVVLSO in Pontormo's, are typical of picture-inscriptions of the emblematic type so popular in the Cinquecento: they add to the significance of the picture, but do so as it were *ab extra*; they are not part of the subject, but comments upon it.

[1] See Karl Frey, *Der Literarische Nachlass Giorgio Vasaris* (Munich, 1923), pp. 17-18.
[2] *Virtus* for *Virtutum* must, it seems, be a mistake of the copyist; the MS in which the letter survives is a transcript.

25. Vasari, *Lorenzo de' Medici il Magnifico*: Florence, Uffizi.

In most of the examples we have so far looked at, the picture-inscription has consisted of no more than a word or two, or at most a line or two, of verse or of prose, usually a familiar phrase or motto. Sometimes, however, the written element bulks larger; the inscription may even take the form of a set of verses composed to celebrate the subject of the painting or specially to be included in it. In such cases it is hard, as it is with the 'emblematic' motto, to fuse the image and the inscription into an aesthetic unity; there is a danger that they will remain disparate, like a literary text and the picture that is meant to illustrate it.

Such are the verses inscribed on the famous pair of portraits by Piero della Francesca, now in the Uffizi, of Federigo, Count of Urbino, and his wife, Battista Sforza. On one side of each of these panels is a bust in profile, on the other side a chariot in which the subject is being drawn in triumph, the Count by white horses, the Countess by unicorns. Below each of these *trionfi* is a Sapphic stanza cut in Roman capitals on a stone panel. These stanzas celebrate the fame of the Count and Countess in conventional terms, in keeping with the painter's Roman images; they must have been composed by a contemporary versifier of the Court of Urbino.[1] These verses are more closely related to the subject-matter of the pictures they accompany than are Vasari's mottoes, but they are just as far from producing a single, complex emotional effect. They run parallel, as it were, to the representation, repeating in verse-language, dully and without distinction, what the painter has said clearly in line and colour. Their true function—and they perform it almost as well for the spectator who does not know Latin as for him who does—is close to that of the inscriptions in Mantegna's Ovetari frescoes: it is simply to reinforce the classicism of the whole representation; we feel, as with an architectural inscription on a Vitruvian entablature, that it is fitting that fine Latin words, whatever their precise significance, should accompany so classical a composition.

In the last years of the fifteenth century, Perugino, working in his native city, produced a composition that combined classical images with original verses, like the little pair of *trionfi* that Piero had painted for his noble patrons at Urbino some fifty years before, but on a much grander scale. Being called upon to decorate the Sala d'Udienza of the Collegio del Cambio, a guild or company who administered justice in Perugia and were responsible for maintaining the

[1] See A. Cinquini, *Il Codice Vaticano Urbinate Latino 1193: Documenti et appunti per la storia letteraria d'Italia nel quattrocento* (n.d.); and *De vita et morte illustris D. Baptistae Sfortiae Comitissae Urbini* (Rome, 1905). Also J. Dennistoun, *Memoirs of the Dukes of Urbino*, ed. E. Hutton (1909), I, 216.

standard of its currency, he executed this commission—perhaps with the help of his young pupil Raphael—by covering the walls and ceiling of the modest audience chamber with frescoes. Over the entrance stands Cato, the model of a virtuous citizen, and facing it are two religious scenes, the Nativity and the Transfiguration; on the right-hand wall, behind the seat of Justice, the Almighty raises his right hand in benediction over a throng of Prophets and Sibyls (Plate 26); while on the left, to meet the eyes of the Collegio in session on the Bench and remind them of the virtues required by their office, are two pairs of allegorical figures, representing Wisdom and Justice, Temperance and Courage (Plate 27). These civic Virtues sit enthroned among the clouds, each attended by a pair of cherubs holding a classical tablet over the heads of three heroic figures standing on the ground beneath them, exponents of the Virtues represented.

Into each of these frescoes Perugino introduced appropriate inscriptions. Across the sky of the Transfiguration are written in golden letters the words *Hic est filius meus dilectus* and *Bonum est nobis hic esse*; while *Gloria in excelsis Deo* trembles in the air above the singing angels of the Nativity, and the Prophets and Sibyls carry in their hands sinuous scrolls that wind about their bodies, disclosing cryptic fragments of mystical and prophetic texts—*Ecce virgo concipiet*, *Veritas de terra*, *Vivificabit mortuos*. To accompany his pagan frescoes, on the other hand, Perugino had recourse, like Piero della Francesca, to pseudo-classical verses: beneath the figure of Cato, and on each of the four *tabellae*, is a set of elegiacs composed for him by a contemporary court poet of Perugia, Francesco Maturanzio.[1]

These frescoes of Perugino provide a paradigm of Renaissance picture-inscriptions, in their texts, in the way they are presented, and in their effect upon the spectator.

The inscriptions that accompany the New Testament scenes and the Old Testament figures are 'labels' belonging to types familiar in ecclesiastical art. In the Nativity and the Transfiguration the texts appearing supernaturally in the air consist of words uttered on the occasions represented; you must recognise them as such if you are to appreciate their effectiveness; when you

---

[1] It may be that Maturanzio not only supplied the verses for Perugino but also suggested to him the Virtues and their exponents, founding himself on an illuminated MS of Cicero's *de Officiis* still preserved in the Biblioteca Civica of Perugia (see Raffaello Marchesi, *Il Cambio di Perugia*, Prato (1853), pp. 356-60).

26. Perugino, *The Eternal Father with Prophets and Sibyls*: Perugia, Collegio del Cambio.

27. Perugino, *Wisdom and Justice*: Perugia, Collegio del Cambio.

do, they simply add a confirmatory stroke to the pictorial description of the scene. The scrolls of the Sibyls and the Prophets are labels of a less obvious kind; the figures are already identified by their names written on the ground beneath them, and the texts they carry are fragmentary and obscure; their precise meaning hardly matters; the broken sentences serve simply to suggest the prophetic powers and sphinx-like utterance of the mystic company.

In the pagan frescoes—Cato and the Virtues—the inscriptions are of a different kind and fulfil a very different purpose. The texts are unfamiliar—indeed, as we have seen, they were composed for the occasion—and compared with those in the other frescoes they are lengthy and elaborate. You cannot take them in at a glance; if you study them, you are distracted from the picture; and you learn from them nothing that affects your feelings about it. Though formally incorporated in the scene, they are really no more a part of it than Piero's verses are a part of the *trionfi* that they accompany; like Piero's verses, they tell the same story as the picture, but in another medium.

Perugino's presentation of the Virtues proves, like Piero's *trionfi*, how hard it is for a painter to make a literary text an integral part of a visual composition. An even clearer illustration of this difficulty is provided by Domenico Ghirlandaio in the *Adoration of the Shepherds* that he painted for the Sassetti chapel in S. Trinità in Florence (Plate 28).

Ghirlandaio's picture shows how completely Renaissance artists, when they treated religious themes either in poetry or in paint, would conflate the pagan with the Christian, the classical with the contemporary, and history with legend.

A curious duplicity of time and place pervades the picture; the setting is Palestine in Italy, and the architecture is of today and yesterday; the manger before which the Child is laid takes the form of a classical sarcophagus; the thatched roof that covers the shed of the Nativity is supported by fluted columns with Corinthian capitals, one of which is clearly inscribed with the date MCCCCLXXXV; and the faces of the shepherds proclaim them, as clearly as do the clothes they are wearing, to be contemporaries of the artist.

Two inscriptions are prominent, one in the background, one in the foreground of the composition. While the Virgin kneels, with eyes downcast, in adoration of the Child, Joseph looks up and away, his hand to his forehead;

73

28. Domenico Ghirlandaio, *The Adoration of the Shepherds*: Florence, S. Trinità.

he is evidently struck with amazement by the star from the East, which has come to rest above the spot; and his gaze carries our attention to the long cavalcade of the Magi, which winds its way round the brow of a distant hill (where the shepherds, still watching their flocks, are being surprised by a herald angel) and passes under a classical arch that bears the legend

GN POMPEIO MAGNO HIRCANVS PONT. P.

As Saxl pointed out in his interpretation of the picture,[1] the arch is a correctly designed triumphal arch and Hircanus was a historical figure, a High Priest whom Pompey reinstated in his office after capturing Jerusalem in 63 B.C.; but the practice of erecting triumphal arches had in fact hardly begun at that date, and the idea that Hircanus erected such a monument in gratitude to Pompey is as much a fiction as is the inscription recording the supposed event. Very probably, both were inventions of Bartolomeo della Fonte, the humanist friend and adviser of Francesco Sassetti, for whom the picture was painted. Della Fonte may well have been responsible also for the elegiac couplet inscribed on the sarcophagus in the foreground, which is the most prominent object in the picture:

ENSE CADENS SOLYMO POMPEI FVLVIVS AVGVR
NVMEN AIT QVAE ME CONTEGIT VRNA DABIT

The augur Fulvius is a character unknown to history; the couplet assumes that this imaginary person was one of the attackers killed in the siege of Jerusalem, and tells us that, as he perished, he prophesied that a god would be given to the world from the tomb that covered him—again, the incident, like the lines recording it, is a pseudo-classical invention.

According to Saxl, the inscription on the triumphal arch indicates the triumph of paganism over Judaism, while the couplet on the sarcophagus signifies the victory of Christianity over the pagan world. 'I do not know', Saxl continues, 'of any obvious connection between the history of Pompey and the coming of Christ, and it would therefore seem that Fontius' interest in the famous Roman caused him to invent the two inscriptions which, through the history of Pompey, interconnect the history of the three great religions. This', he concludes, 'is the purpose of the classical details which form a strange

[1] In his article already quoted, *The Journal of the Warburg and Courtauld Institutes*, IV (1941), 19–46.

contrast to the figures of the landscape in Ghirlandaio's picture. Only the spectator who understands the meaning of the ruins, the sacred figures and those who surround them, grasps the full content of the miracle of the Nativity as Sassetti and Fontius conceived it.'

Renaissance critics no doubt looked at Ghirlandaio's *Adoration* with the double vision that I spoke of at the beginning of this lecture; they were able to take in the pseudo-classical inscription on the arch and the unfamiliar couplet on the sarcophagus and to see the scene presented by the painter in the light of their implications. We find this difficult to do. It is with Ghirlandaio's inscriptions as it is with the 'emblematic' inscriptions in Pontormo's and Vasari's portraits: however much they impressed or moved their contemporaries, they leave us cold as we look today at the pictures that contain them; the artist failed to unite text with image, and the inscription remains no more than an appendage or an ornament.

This is not always so; it is not so, I think, with the three pictures that I now proceed to deal with. In each of these an inscription plays a leading part; until we understand it we cannot fully take the picture in; and once we have understood it, its meaning remains united in our minds with the visual image.

The first of these is a picture by Moretto[1] in the Pinacotheca Tosio-Martinengo in Brescia (Plate 29); its subject is something of a mystery.[2] It represents a young woman of appealing beauty, resting her left arm on a stone ledge and holding a golden sceptre in her hand; her elaborately plaited hair is braided with a string of pearls; a rich fur robe, falling across one shoulder, leaves her neck three-quarters bare; and she looks almost timidly at the

---

[1] Moretto seems to have been addicted to Latin inscriptions, though—to judge from the spellings NOSSTER and ESSTIMABATVR, on one of the scrolls belonging to his series of prophets in the Church of S. Giovanni Evangelista in Brescia—he cannot himself have been much of a Latinist.

In his *Virgin and Child appearing to SS. Hippolytus and Catherina*, in the National Gallery, the Saints are identified by label-inscriptions containing their names on *cartellini*, and Moretto places in the foreground, between the two martyrs, a stone resembling a Roman altar, with the inscription MEMBRIS DISSOLVI VOLVERVNT NE VINCVLIS DIVELLERENTVR AETERNIS.

In a *Deposition* painted in 1554 (now in the Metropolitan Museum, New York) there are incised on a stone at the feet of the dead Christ the words FACTVS EST OBEDIENS VSQVE AD MORTEM—in which critics have seen a premonition of the artist's own death, which took place before the end of the year.

[2] The tradition that the picture represents Tullia d'Aragona, a famous Roman courtesan of the period, is apparently to be traced to Count Tosio, who acquired the picture from a convent in 1829; it was accepted uncritically by Guido Biagi in *Una Etera romana* (Florence, 1897). See P. Molmenti, *Il Moretto da Brescia* (Florence, 1898), p. 107, and G. Gombosi, *Moretto da Brescia* (Basel, 1943), p. 110.

QVAE SAG...ICANIS
CAPVT SALTANDO
OBTINVIT

29. Moretto da Brescia, *Salome*: Brescia, Pinacotheca Tosio-Martinengo.

spectator, with parted lips and modest eyes. On the stone upon which she is leaning is cut, in bold Roman capitals, the legend

QVAE SACRVM IOANIS

CAPVT SALTANDO

OBTINVIT

The picture, then, is in some sense a representation of Salome; but one does not have to look at it for long to see that it must be at the same time the portrait of an actual person—dressed up, perhaps, to take part in a pageant or masquerade.[1] This sense of ambiguity is heightened by the phrasing of the inscription and by the manner in which the artist has chosen to present it: the words tell us who the subject 'is', but they convey their information obliquely, and they are so placed on the stone ledge that she herself is unaware of them.

Beside Moretto's picture we may set a more familiar work—Lotto's *Lucrezia* in the National Gallery (Plate 30). Here too there is a certain artificiality about the presentation of the sitter: 'One cannot help feeling', says Berenson, 'that the artist was not persuaded of the lady's sincerity, and that he would certainly not have given her this pose and these accessories if she had not asked for them.'[2] Like Moretto's Salome, she is clad in a rich robe and her head is elaborately dressed; her principal 'accessory' is a drawing of Lucretia in the act of suicide, which she holds at arm's length in her left hand while she points with her right forefinger to a piece of paper lying on the table beside her. On the paper are written, in clear Roman capitals, the dying words attributed to Lucretia by Livy:[3]

NEC VLLA IMPVDICA LV

CRETIAE EXEMPLO VIVET

In both these pictures the sitters are very deliberately posed, each contains a Latin inscription, and each inscription identifies the sitter with a woman famous

[1] She is, in the words of Venturi (*Storia dell'Arte Italiana*, Hoepli, 1929, IX, iv, p. 195), 'non la danzatrice, ma una donzella con poca vita; non la tragica portatrice della testa recisa, ma una reginetta da commedia, che niuno riconoscerebbe se non si appoggiasse al marmo con l'iscrizione dichiaratrice del esser suo'.

[2] *Lorenzo Lotto*, 'Complete Edition' (Phaidon, 1956), p. 99.

[3] I. lvii. 10, quoted by Boccaccio, *De mulieribus claris*, c. xlvi, which may have been the source from which Lotto, or whoever supplied him with it, derived the quotation. The words do not mean that Lucretia's example will ensure that henceforth no woman shall survive the loss of her honour; they mean that no woman who in the future wishes to go on living after she has lost her honour will be able to appeal to Lucretia's case as a precedent.

30. Lotto, *Lucrezia*: London, The National Gallery.

in history. It is tempting to suggest that there might be some connection between the two works—that both were records of the same occasion, perhaps a Masque of Fair Women or some similar festivity. Such an occasion might have occurred at Bergamo in the late 1520s: both Lotto[1] and Moretto[2] were working in S. Maria Maggiore in that city between 1526 and 1529; it is to 1529–30 that Berenson (*Lotto*, 1955, p.133), on grounds of style, would assign Lotto's *Lucrezia*, and the costume in the picture (see The National Gallery's Catalogue, *The Sixteenth Century Venetian School* (by Cecil Gould, 1959), p.54) 'unequivocally indicates a date around the year 1530'.

[1] See Venturi, *Storia dell'Arte Italiana*, IX, iv, p. 2, quoting from documents in the Archivio of S. Maria Maggiore, Bergamo.

[2] See G. Gombosi, *Moretto da Brescia* (Basel, 1943), p. 84, quoting from documents in the Biblioteca Civica, Bergamo ('Fabricae chori et Reformationis factae', fo. 75). Gombosi would, however, date the *Salome*, presumably on grounds of style, in the late 1530s or early 1540s.

We may be uncertain about the full significance of Moretto's quotation, but both he and Lotto have succeeded in uniting their inscriptions with the images that they accompany; the text, in each case, is not simply a title or a comment or an appendix: its message is a part of the picture.

The same is true of the inscription in a more famous work—the portrait in the Accademia in Venice called *La Vecchia* (Plate 31), attributed to Giorgione and hung near his *Tempesta*. Here too the subject looks out at us over a stone ledge; but the stone is unlettered, and the words of the inscription—COL TEMPO—appear on a scroll protruding from her sleeve.

The script in which the words COL TEMPO are written is oddly irregular; the vowels are very much smaller than the consonants, and the writing does not follow the convolutions of the scroll, which is tucked into the old woman's sleeve in a most unnatural fashion. All this unrealism is surely meant to convey to us that the words are not an actual written message that La Vecchia is carrying; they represent a thought that is passing through her mind. Unlike Moretto's Salome, she is well aware of the meaning of the message, and her pointing finger emphasises its application to herself. If the scroll were plucked from her sleeve and the words it carries were engraved instead, as it were in another dimension, upon the parapet in front of her (as they are in Moretto's Salome inscription), then the message would come from the painter and not from his subject, and something would be drained away from the effect of her gesture and her expression.

The inscription in *La Vecchia* is brief, familiar, evocative—almost necessary attributes of an inscription, if it is to be fully integrated into a picture and to contribute to its pervading mood. I know of no Renaissance picture that achieves this effect as successfully as do two pictures painted in the seventeenth century: Poussin's pastoral idylls *Et in Arcadia Ego*.

Panofsky, in a classic essay on these pictures,[1] traces the history of the quotation from its unknown origin and explains the differing interpretations that have been put upon it. Strictly, *Et* should be taken closely with *in Arcadia*: 'Even in Arcadia, I [am present]'; the implication is a grim one, often made

---

[1] 'Et in Arcadia Ego: Poussin and the Elegiac Tradition', in *Meaning and the Visual Arts* (Doubleday Anchor Books, New York, 1957), pp. 295–320; originally published under a slightly different title in *Philosophy and History, Essays presented to Ernst Cassirer* (Oxford, 1936).

31. Giorgione (*attrib.*), *La Vecchia*: Venice, Accademia.

32. Poussin, *Et in Arcadia Ego*: Devonshire Collection, Chatsworth House, Derbyshire.

explicit by some emblem of mortality: it is Death that is speaking, to tell us that his writ runs even in Arcadia. But the words were very frequently given a different interpretation, and sometimes they were transposed ('Et ego in Arcadia') so as to make that interpretation easier: *Et* is then taken with *ego*— 'I too [have lived] in Arcadia'—the imagined speaker is one who has been exiled by fate, or by death, from the happy regions, and the tone of his utterance is nostalgic.

In 1625 or thereabouts Poussin painted his first version of a pastoral inspired by this theme, a picture now at Chatsworth (Plate 32). A group of shepherds, in a grove, are confronted by a death's-head that grins at them from a marble plinth; they recoil in astonishment, perplexity, and horror. It is clear how the words engraved upon the stone are to be interpreted; their realisation of what those words imply is the subject of the picture, and the words themselves are perfectly expressive of its mood.

Half a dozen years later, Poussin painted another version of *Et in Arcadia Ego*, now in the Louvre (Plate 33). Here, the shepherds are gathered round a classical monument, and one of them is evidently spelling out to his companions the legend engraved upon it. The death's-head has disappeared; a pensive melancholy pervades the scene. If Poussin had been a more sensitive Latinist, he would have altered the order of the words. Even as it is, there can be no doubt how the shepherd is interpreting them: they are the utterance of one who, speaking from the grave, declares that he, or she, was also once an inhabitant of Arcady.

Et in Arcadia Ego—each of Poussin's pictures, in its own way, perfectly expresses the mood and meaning of the equivocal inscription that provides its title and its subject.

If I pursued further the history of the picture-inscription, I should be taken outside the scope of this lecture. As the humanistic enthusiasm for classical inscriptions lost its freshness, the painter's use of the epigraph became more calculated and more literary, closer to the use made of it by those who devised mottoes for emblems, and more dependent for its effect upon the quickness of the observer's wit.[1]

[1] A late-sixteenth-century example of a witty picture-inscription is provided by the portrait of John Donne recently discovered by Mr John Bryson in the Lothian collection at Newbattle Abbey. In his

In the eighteenth century a distinguished critic called attention to the possibility of using inscriptions so as to add a literary element to an architectural composition. Diderot, in his *Salons*,[1] describes a rustic scene, with peasants discovered among classical ruins, and deplores the fact that the ruins are uninscribed. 'Pourquoi ne lit-on pas', he asks, 'en manière d'enseigne, au dessus de ces marchandes d'herbes,

DIVO AVGVSTO, DIVO NERONI?

Pourquoi n'avoir pas gravé sur cet obélisque

JOVI SERVATORI, QVOD FELICITER PERICVLVM EVASERIT, SYLLA?

ou TRIGESIES CENTENIS MILLIBVS HOMINVM CAESIS, POMPEIVS?

Cette dernière inscription reveillerait en moi l'horreur que je dois à un monstre qui se fait gloire d'avoir égorgé trois millions d'hommes. Ces ruines me parleraient.' The ruins of Pompey's triumphal arch, so inscribed, would have spoken for Diderot as they did for Ghirlandaio, but with a more sophisticated voice.

The inscription, promising immortality, that is itself crumbling to dust with the marble on which it is inscribed has provided a theme for poets and moralists both before and since Diderot. Pope gave it a pictorial turn in the frontispiece he designed for his *Essay on Man* (1722), which shows a grey-beard blowing bubbles amidst the ruins of the Capitol;[2] ROMA AETERNA is inscribed upon the remnants of the Coliseum; VIRO IMMORTALI on the plinth of a statue that has broken and fallen to the ground; CAPITOLI IMMOBILE SAXVM on the base of a truncated column. The irony is carried a stage further in a painting[3] based on Pope's design (Plate 34), which shows a

will, by which he left the picture to his friend Sir Robert Ker, Donne described it as 'taken in shadows'; it represents him against a dark background 'with folded arms and melancholy hat'; and the inscription round its upper rim—ILLVMINA TENEBRAS NOSTRAS DOMINA—makes explicit, by an irreverent parody of the third Collect for Evensong, the fact that Donne is here playing the part of the melancholy lover: to deprive the picture of that legend would be to blunt the point of its intention. For a full account of the portrait, the circumstances of its discovery, and the significance of its 'properties', see Mr Bryson's article in *The Times*, 13 October 1959.

[1] *Salon de* 1767; *Œuvres*, ed. J. Assézat, XI (Paris, 1876), pp. 247–8.

[2] The drawing is reproduced as the frontispiece to Professor Maynard Mack's edition of the *Essay* in the Twickenham edition of Pope's Poems (Methuen, 1950).

[3] Now in the possession of Miss Caroline Newton of Berwyn, Pennsylvania. It is not known who painted this picture or whom the figure in the foreground is supposed to represent. Its history and significance are discussed by Professor Mack, *op. cit.* p. xc.

33. Poussin, *Et in Arcadia Ego*: Paris, Louvre.

figure in the foreground holding in his hand a paper that partly obscures the inscription on the base of the column, so that it cuts off from view the first two letters of the word IMMOBILE.

Those who imagine that the transmutation of IMMOBILE to MOBILE is fortuitous should compare Hogarth's picture (Plate 35) of the painful preacher discoursing on the text 'Come unto me all ye that labour and are heavy laden and I will give you rest' to a slumbering auditory; conspicuous among them is a handsome young woman dozing with her prayer-book open on her lap at a page—*Of Matrimony*—that shows clearly what it is that she is dreaming of, while the Royal Motto blazoned on the wall plainly indicates the prevailing devotional temperature: its first word is occluded, and only the words ET MON DROIT are visible to the eye of the spectator.

To use an inscription in a picture so that its effectiveness depends upon its being in part invisible, and the significant word the word that is not seen,

85

34. *Allegorical scene in the Forum*: Miss Caroline Newton's Collection, Berwyn, Pennsylvania.

35. Hogarth, *The Sleeping Congregation*, 1736.

implies a degree of sophistication in the artist more in keeping with the wit of the Baroque epigraphists than with the enthusiasm of the humanists of the Renaissance.[1]

THE INSCRIPTION IN MONUMENTAL ART

Though an inscription may be thought to be an alien and intrusive element in a picture, of a monument it is a natural and almost a necessary part; for the purpose of a monument is to tell or to remind us about somebody or something, and since the sculptor's or architect's forms are not usually able by themselves to do this in satisfying measure, they must be supplemented with words: the tomb requires an epitaph; the memorial, a text announcing who or what it is that it commemorates.

Here again, as with the inscription in a picture, arises the problem of how to unite the text with its setting: the monumental inscription should not be unduly prominent; on the other hand it must not be swamped by its architectural and sculptural surroundings. The feature that carries the inscription must not be disproportionately large, and the text itself must not be prolix. It must not too long detain the eye or distract attention from the main design.

We have seen that in the Middle Ages most monumental inscriptions when they were not in verse were little more than conventional formulae, and that in the middle of the fifteenth century the verse epitaph seems to have gone out of fashion. And I have pointed out that it was not until well into the sixteenth century that the prose inscription became lineated, i.e. that epigraphists habitually composed inscriptions with a view to their text being set out by the stone-cutter in lines that enhanced its significance by means of variations in their length.

I suspect that the increasing frequency of lineation in sixteenth-century inscriptions was causally connected with a change in the part played by the inscription itself as an element in monumental design.

Critics and art historians have analysed very fully the sculpture and design

---

[1] A similar effect may be achieved undesignedly. Until the other day, a number of displaced tombstones were to be seen, or half seen, in the churchyard of St Peter in the East in Oxford, leaning one on top of another against a wall. One of them (of the early nineteenth century) was so covered that only the first words of the epitaph were visible: '*Beneath this Monitor of Human Instability...*' The Monitor itself has now disappeared completely.

of Renaissance monuments[1] and experts in calligraphy have paid attention to the lettering of the inscriptions to be found on them,[2] but I know of no study devoted to the part played by the inscription in monumental art. The field is a wide one, and so richly stocked with examples that it is dangerous to generalise—it is so easy for the proponent of any theory to support it with instances, so easy for the critic to find evidence that seems to contradict it. Statements true about Florence may not hold in Rome, and statements true about Rome may not hold in Venice; the existence of 'schools' and the influence of individual artists have to be reckoned with, and conclusions based on unverified impressions are liable to be refuted by the statistical results of detailed enquiry.

What one needs is a comprehensive catalogue of the principal inscribed monuments produced in Italy between 1300 and 1600, showing the type of each monument and inscription, the date when it was made, the place it belongs to, and the artist or artists responsible for it.[3] Until some such survey is available, one can make only the most tentative suggestions, and I offer the following account simply as a possible explanation of the evidence as it presents itself to me.

In the Middle Ages, as we have seen, the monumental inscription usually took the form either of a more or less conventional formula, or else of a set of elegiac or panegyrical verses. Either of these—provided, in the latter case, that the elegy or panegyric was not too long—could be strung out continuously along a strip that ran round the ledge of a sarcophagus or altar tomb or the perimeter of a floor-slab, with no attempt at display and (of course) no possibility of lineation. That is perhaps the most familiar form of the mediaeval inscription. A long elegy or panegyric, on the other hand, needed more room; it would normally be inscribed on a rectangular stone without any regard to division into metrical lines. The tablet would not form an integral part of the design of the monument, but would lurk on a recessed surface or be placed, separately, on the wall near by.

[1] I am especially indebted to the chapters dealing with monumental art in Mr John Pope-Hennessy's series of works on Mediaeval and Renaissance Sculpture in Italy.
[2] See the authorities enumerated in my footnote on p. 13.
[3] Voluminous notes for an intended Corpus of Italian Monuments of the twelfth to the sixteenth century were prepared by Miss Margaret Longhurst of the Victoria and Albert Museum, but were left unfinished at her death. These notes were edited by Mr Ian Lowe and a limited edition was printed for Miss

I suspect that it was the rediscovery of the classical Roman forms of letter—so much more beautiful, and so much easier to read at a distance, than any mediaeval script—that led to the change in fashion that seems to have taken place just half way through the century. The sculptor who made the monument, being assured of fine Roman lettering, was glad to display an inscription as part of his design. The epigraphist, for his part, would compose his text with a view to its being so displayed; he was no longer simply writing an elegy to be preserved in stone instead of upon parchment; he was consciously contributing to a work of visual art. The invention of typography just at this time no doubt helped on the process of diverting the verse elegy from the marble of the monument by providing an alternative, and at least equally effectual, means of preserving and publicising it.

It was for the architect or sculptor to determine how prominent a place in the monument should be allotted to the inscription, and how it should be worked into the general design. Sometimes the text would be entirely subordinate, being engraved on a convenient panel or even on the convex and curving surface of the side of a sarcophagus (Antonio Rossellino's monument of the Cardinal of Portugal in S. Miniato al Monte (c. 1461) (Plate 36) is a good example); sometimes it would be introduced upon a scroll or banner forming an intimate part of the sculptural design, as in Bernardo Rossellino's monument of the Beata Villana in S. Maria Novella (1451) (Plate 37) or Amadeo's monument of Medea Colleoni in the Colleoni Chapel in Bergamo (c. 1471) (Plate 38); more often it would be cut on a tablet obviously introduced into the design in order to receive it; such a tablet might be modestly accommodated to its setting, as in Bernardo Rossellino's Bruni monument in S. Croce (1444) (Plate 8) or Desiderio da Settignano's monument of Carlo Marsuppini (Plate 39), also in S. Croce (1459); or it might occupy a prominent, or dominant, place in the design, as in Agostino di Duccio's Arca degli Antenati in the Tempio Malatestiano, Rimini (c. 1450), the monument of Marcantonio Albertoni in S. Maria del Popolo in Rome (1485), Matteo Civitali's monument of S. Romano, S. Romano, Lucca (1490), or the monument of Lorenzo Gerusino in S. Margherita in Rome (1498) (Plates 40–43).

Longhurst's executors as an 'exchange publication' for the Museum. They are a valuable guide; but, apart from their inchoate state, they by no means invariably record or describe the inscriptions on the monuments included.

90

36. Antonio Rossellino, Monument of the Cardinal of Portugal:
Florence, S. Miniato al Monte, c. 1461.

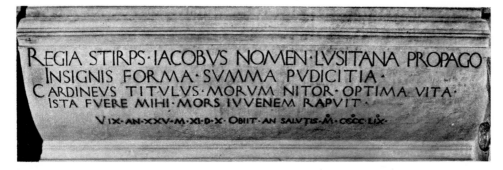

REGIA STIRPS·IACOBVS NOMEN·LVSITANA PROPAGO
INSIGNIS FORMA·SVMMA PVDICITIA·
CARDINEVS TITVLVS MORVM NITOR OPTIMA VITA·
ISTA FVERE MIHI·MORS IVVENEM RAPVIT·
VIX·AN·XXV·M·XI·D·X· OBIIT AN SALVTIS·M̄·CCCC·LIX·

Detail from Plate 36.

When his text achieved such prominence, the epigraphist would be tempted to spread himself and write at inordinate length, with results to be seen in such monuments as Rizzo's Tron monument in the Frari in Venice or Pietro Lombardo's Mocenigo monument in SS. Giovanni e Paolo (after 1476). Lengthy monumental inscriptions are not satisfactory; faced with a considerable piece of prose or verse as part of a complex sculptural design, the spectator is pulled in one direction by the sculptor, and in another by the epigraphist; each distracts him from enjoyment of the other's work. The epigraphist who has much to say may prefer to say it on his own; while the sculptor does not want the attention of his potential admirers to be detached and detained, either by the contents of a public notice or by the beauties of a verse elegy or of a piece of elaborately lineated prose.

So, it seems, in the course of the sixteenth century, the close union between the sculptor and the epigraphist was dissolved, and the inscription-tablet, detaching itself from the sepulchral or commemorative monument, achieved autonomy and appeared more and more frequently alone, sometimes (classical Rome providing a precedent) surmounted by a plaque or bust, e.g. the Ponzetti monument in S. Maria della Pace in Rome (1505) (Plate 44) and the Bembo monument in S. Antonio in Padua (1547) (Plate 45), sometimes surrounded by sculptured ornament—a type familiar in English churches.

When his text had thus shaken off its architectural accompaniments and stood by itself, the epigraphist may well have felt that his freedom to exploit the possibilities of lineation, as a means of catching and holding the eye of the observer and bringing out the finer shades of his own intention, was more extensive than it could be when he was contributing a subordinate part to a visual artistic whole.

It was in these conditions, in the course of the sixteenth century, that the lineated inscription became in Italy a recognised literary form. My survey of the part played by epigraphy in the various fields of Renaissance art, summary and superficial though it is, will have shown how thoroughly architects, painters, and sculptors had prepared the public to appreciate this new phase in its development.

OSSA . VILLANE . MVLIERIS . SANCTISSIME
IN . HOC . CELEBRI . TVMVLO . REQVIESCVNT

37. Bernardo Rossellino, Monument of the Beata Villana: Florence, S. Maria Novella, 1451.

38. Giovanni Antonio Amadeo, Monument of Medea Colleoni: Bergamo, Colleoni Chapel, *c.* 1471.

39. Desiderio da Settignano, Monument of Carlo Marsuppini: Florence, S. Croce, 1459.

The inscription on the tomb reads:

SIGISMVNDVS
PANDVLFVS
MALATESTA
PANDVLFI · F
INGENTIBVS
MERITIS · PROBIT
ATIS · FORTITV
DINIS · QVE · ILLV
TRI · GENERIS · VO
MAIORIBVS · PO
STERIS · QVE ·

40. Agostino di Duccio, Arca degli Antenati: Rimini, Tempio Malatestiano, c. 1450.

MARCO ANTONII EQVITIS ROMANI
FILIO EX NOBILI ALBERTONVM FAMILIA
CORPORE ANIMO Q INSIGNI
QVI ANNVM AGENS XXX
PESTE INGVINARIA INTERIIT
AN SALVTIS CHRISTIANAE
M CCCC LXXXV DIE XXII IVLII
HEREDES B M P

41. Monument of Marcantonio Albertoni: Rome, S. Maria del Popolo, 1485.

42. Matteo Civitali, Monument of S. Romano: Lucca, S. Romano, 1490.

43. Monument of Lorenzo Gerusino: Rome, S. Margherita, 1498.

D O M
BEATRICI ET LAVINIAE PONZETTIS
INDOLIS FESTIVITATISQ
ADMIRANDAE QVAS NEAPOLIS
TVLIT ROMA PROBE EDVCAVIT
PESTILENTIA QVAE DESIISSE
FEREBATVR VNA DIE ABSVMPSIT
VIXER HAEC VI ILLA ANN VIII
FERNANDVS PATRVVS APOSTOLICI
FISCI VII VIR DECANVS MAGNO
SOLATIO SPEQ ORBATVS
DELITIIS ANIMVLISQVE
SVIS MOERENS POSVIT
V KL DECEMBR M D V

44. Monument of Beatrice and Lavinia Ponzetti: Rome, S. Maria della Pace, 1505.

45. Michele Sanmicheli, Monument of Pietro Bembo: Padua, S. Antonio, 1547.

III

THE INSCRIPTION AS
A LITERARY FORM

In my last lecture I discussed the inscription as an element in architectural
compositions, in paintings, and in sepulchral and other monuments. I took my
examples from Italy, where the study and the production of inscriptions
flourished most profusely, and I tried to show how large a part the inscription
played in the art of the Italian Renaissance, and to trace the process by which
the written 'legend' increased in importance as an element in memorial
monuments; how the plaque or tablet that carried it tended to be given a more
and more prominent place in the composition, and increasing attention came
to be paid to the design and execution of its lettering; and how it ultimately
broke free from its architectural and sculptural accompaniments and acquired
a literary and artistic importance of its own.

A representative collection of fifteenth-century memorials would consist of
elaborate monuments comprising sculptured figures in architectural settings;[1]
a gallery of typical sixteenth-century examples would consist mainly of
inscribed mural tablets or plaques, often surrounded with sculptural decora-
tion, and sometimes surmounted by a bust.

It seems reasonable to suppose that this shift of emphasis was due to economic
and social, as well as to artistic, causes: perhaps in the society of the time there
was an expanding class of persons rich and important enough to be commemorated, but not important enough to be commemorated at the public
expense and not rich enough to afford an elaborate architectural monument;
the mural tablet or inscribed floor-slab exactly met their needs. One can also,
I think, trace an increasing secularisation in the monumental art of the time,
which may reflect a corresponding movement in society: a larger proportion

[1] See, for example, the plates illustrating *Das Italienische Grabmal der Frührenaissance*, by Paul Schubring
(Berlin, 1904).

of the persons commemorated are laymen, and the texts of memorial inscriptions became at once more personal and less ecclesiastical.

By the beginning of the seventeenth century the inscription had come into its own; elaborate sculptured monuments were still of course produced (in Britain, always a century behind the times in such matters, the monumental art flourished then as never before), but in most memorials the inscription was the dominant feature. And it was a natural consequence of this—because the eye of the spectator was now focused on the text—that epigraphists should have given special thought to the form their words were to assume in upon the stone, so that the lineated inscription became a recognised type of literary composition.

In this lecture I shall trace the inscription through the next stage of its evolution, and show how after it had achieved, as it were, an independent existence, the lapidary epigraph ceased to be lapidary, breaking away from the stone and transferring itself to cheaper and less substantial materials, fixing itself upon paper, and finally becoming a kind of book.

INSCRIPTIONS FOR 'MACHINAE'

A factor that favoured this development of lapidary writing was the custom of erecting temporary monuments on important occasions—the pageant or the marriage or funeral ceremony, the celebration of the birth of a royal infant or an imperial or episcopal visit, the festival marking an anniversary or a treaty or a triumph. For such occasions an Italian city would prepare an elaborate architectural display: triumphal arches, temples, theatres, processional vehicles, catafalques and other *machinae* or *apparatus* would be manufactured out of stucco, pasteboard, painted wood or canvas and lavishly decorated with allegorical figures, emblems, coats of arms and inscriptions (Plate 46). The inscriptions would usually be in Latin, and in prose; sometimes in verse, and sometimes, but less often, in Italian. Like the rest of the *apparatus*, the inscriptions were intended to attract and hold the attention of the spectator, and since they were painted on cheap materials such as wood and canvas, composers did not feel such need for brevity as they did when their words were to be cut upon stone; their texts, therefore, were often extravagantly long (Plate 47).

It was not only in Italy that these *apparatus* were the fashion: they flourished all over Europe; the Emperor Maximilian I had a special taste for such displays, and called in the German humanists and artists of his day to design them.[1]

Here was a vast field for the epigraphist, and throughout Europe for a couple of hundred years a huge crop must have grown up in it.[2] Only a small proportion of this crop has come down to us; the originals must have been broken up and burned with the rest of the apparatus when the pageant was over; some of the texts, however, have been preserved in books of *fêtes*, *pompes funèbres*, and the like, a *genre* that affords material for a recognised branch of book-collecting and bibliography.

'INSCRIPTIONES ARGUTAE'

Another factor that affected the development of the inscription was the fashion of witty writing, or *argutezza*. Even before the beginning of the sixteenth century, composers had begun to infuse into their imitations of classical inscriptions unclassical strains of feeling and turns of expression. The epitaphs of Pontano in his chapel in Naples in the 1490s are among the earliest examples of the effects of this new spirit.

But throughout the sixteenth century the classical model remained dominant. How strong its influence was, one can judge from a controversy that took place at the very end of the century. The parties in the dispute were Battista Guarini, author of *Il Pastor Fido*, and Francesco Pola, of Verona, an epigraphist celebrated in his day.[3] Pola had composed an epitaph on the father and brother of his friend Domenico Cataneo, which fell into the hands of Guarini. Guarini criticised it severely and suggested an alternative version which, he claimed,

[1] For the part played by Dürer in recording a triumphal procession of the Emperor see K. Giehlow, 'Dürers Entwürfe für das Triumphrelief Kaiser Maximilians I. im Louvre. Eine Studie zur Entwicklungs-geschichte des Triumphzuges', *Jahrbuch des Kunsthistorischen Sammlungen*, XXIX, 1 (Vienna, 1910), pp. 14–84.

[2] A list of more than a hundred published descriptions of funeral displays in various European countries is given by C.-F. Menestrier, S.J., on pp. 19–36 of his *Des Decorations Funebres. Ou il est amplement traité des Tentures, des Lumieres, des Mausolées, Catafalques, Inscriptions, et autres Ornemens funebres* (Paris, 1684). Menestrier's chapter 'Des Inscriptions' (pp. 232–90) opens with the following words: 'Les inscriptions sont la partie la plus essentielle aux Decorations funebres, parce qu'elles en sont l'Ame. Elles appliquent les sujets, font parler les Figures, les Emblêmes et les Devises: Et il n'y a rien en tous ces desseins, où elles n'ayent la meilleure part.'

[3] In 1610 Pola composed inscriptions for the busts of the Doges Tribuno Memmo and Sebastiano Ziani on the façade of S. Giorgio Maggiore in Venice; they were not, however, accepted by the authorities (see A. Da Mosto, *I Dogi di Venezia*, Ongania, Venice, 1939, p. 55).

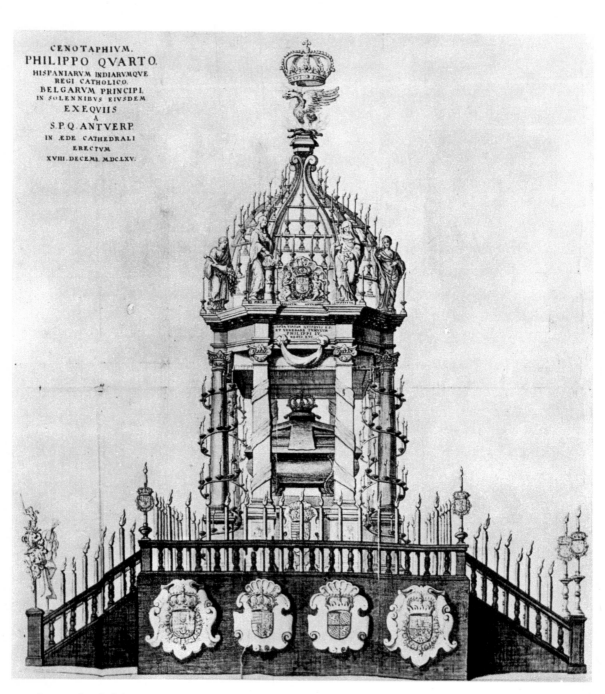

CENOTAPHIVM.
PHILIPPO QVARTO.
HISPANIARVM INDIARVMQVE
REGI CATHOLICO.
BELGARVM PRINCIPI.
IN SOLENNIBVS EIVSDEM
EXEQVIIS
A
S.P.Q. ANTVERP
IN ÆDE CATHEDRALI
ERECTVM
XVIII. DECEMB. MDCLXV.

46. Cenotaph of Philip IV, Antwerp, 1665 (Plantin, 1666).

104

47. Cenotaph of Vittorio Amedeo, Turin, 1637 (G. D. Tarino, 1638).

avoided the faults of which Pola had been guilty. Pola replied with a pamphlet, written in 1597–8, in the form of a dialogue[1] which (according to the publisher of the second edition) was so popular that 'appena fu veduto, che venduto'.

The charge made by Guarini against Pola's epitaph was simply that it broke the capital rule of classical inscriptions, in that it was complex and not concise: 'è di forma moderna', said Guarini, 'percioche gli antichi nelle loro iscrizioni furono tanto sobri e tanto stretti che un sol concetto il più breve, che lor si poteva, se ne spedivano'. To this Pola replied that the style of his epitaph was not 'moderna', that it did not transgress the limits of simplicity and concision prescribed by the ancient Romans, and that Guarini's was itself equally liable to the charges that he levelled at his rival's.

The fact that two distinguished men of letters should have engaged in such a controversy shows what store their contemporaries set upon skill in the composing of inscriptions; the terms of the dispute prove that, while such a thing as a 'forma moderna' had come to be recognised in epigraphy, both the disputants still accepted as the rule a strict conformity to classical models.

The continued prevalence of the classical ideal throughout the sixteenth century is attested by an authority who wrote nearly a century later, Christian Weise, Professor of Poetry and Eloquence at Jena. 'Quicquid…ab aliis tum [i.e. at the end of the sixteenth century] tractabatur, intra simplicem antiquitatis imitationem visum est consistere', says Weise, looking back on that period from the 1670s; and he quotes instances from Belgium (the statue of the Duke of Alba erected in Antwerp in 1571), Italy (the statue of Alessandro Farnese on the Capitol, 1592), and England (the inscriptions on the *machinae gratulatoriae* at the coronation of James I in 1603); in all these, he says, the inscriptions were purely classical (*De Argutis Inscriptionibus*, pp. 90–1). But 'la forma moderna' was already on the way in, and by the end of the seventeenth century a striking change had come over the epigraphic scene.

Weise's *De Argutis Inscriptionibus*, which came out at Weissenfels in 1678,[2] is the classic guide-book to the new epigraphy. Its title-page vividly illustrates the change that had taken place in the course of a century (Plate 48). The emphasis is now on *wit*, or *point* ('argutiae', 'argutezza'). Weise treats his subject as a

---

[1] *L'Epitafio Overo Difesa d'un Epitafio fatto da Francesco Pola Giureconsulto & notato dall'illustre Signor Caualiere Battista Guarini* (Venice, Moretti, 1600; second edition, Verona, 1626).

[2] Reprinted, with the addition of a portrait of the author as frontispiece, at Jena in 1688. My references are to this edition.

M. CHRISTIANUS WEISE
IN AUGUSTEO POLIT. ELOQU. ET
POES. PROF. PUBL.

WEISIUS *hospitium est Eratus, Svada atq;Minerva*
Effigies illud fiftit, at hafce liber.

F. Lipfia
Criiker fc. Jena *L. Ioach. Fellerus. PP.*

CHRISTIANI WEISII
DE POESI
HODIERNORUM POLITICORUM
five
De
ARGUTIS
INSCRIPTIO-
NIBUS
LIBRI II.
Qvorum Prior Naturam, Originem,
Ufum, Auctores & varietatem Infcriptio-
nis; Pofterior facillima imitandi Arti-
ficia perfeqvitur
Additis Clariffimorum Virorum
EXEMPLIS,
In eorum gratiam, qvi vel hodiernum mo-
rem fectari, vel confcribendi carminis com-
pendium qvzrere cupiunt.

Impenfis MATTHÆI BIRCKNERI,
Bibliop. Jenenf. & Helmftad.
J E N Æ,
Ex Chalcographéo GEORGI HEINRICI MÜLLERI.
M. DC. LXXXVIII.

48. Title-page of Christian Weise's *De Argutis Inscriptionibus* (Jena, 1688).

kind of poetry: 'modern political poetry', as he puts it. He explains in his Address to the Reader why he calls his book 'De Poesi Hodiernorum Politicorum'; this is not, he says, because he wishes to suggest that all who concern themselves with politics should take up this kind of writing, but because nowadays notable judgments on affairs of state are commonly cast in this form. Anyone, he says, who keeps his eyes open must have seen inscriptions which deal, in the way either of satire or of panegyric, with the issues of peace and war. And such productions, Weise continues, are none the less poetry for not being metrical; metre is the clothing, not the body, of poetry.

Weise deals with his subject systematically: the first of his two Books covers the theory, the second the practice, of epigraphy. In the first chapter of Book 1 he sets out to define the inscription: Epigraphy is, he says, something between Oratory and Poetry, and the essential mark of the inscription is that each line, or pair of lines, should contain a perfected epigrammatic 'point'. He then traces the origins of the inscription from classical and post-classical Rome,[1] through Renaissance composers such as Pontano,[2] and the sixteenth-century *elogia* of Giovio and Beza—'neque tamen ista Elogia communem Oratoris stylum excedebant, adeoque a nostris argutiis longius erant remoti'—to Justus Lipsius, whom he regards as the father of the witty inscription, *styli argutioris celeberrimus novator*. 'Is', says Weise, 'quo minus Inscriptionum hodiernarum aliqua posuerit fundamenta, nullum est dubium.' He was among the first to 'display' in lineated form the dedications of his books, and among the first of his time 'qui...Arcus triumphales et id genus machinas argutis Inscriptionibus exornavit'.

Such epigraphical displays of wit would never have become popular, according to Weise, 'nisi ultimam obstetricis manum admovisset Jesuitarum societas'. It was the Jesuits, he says, especially in Italy and France, who, 'Disputationum, Theatrorumque monumentorum Parergorum deditissimi... Inscriptionum lusus ita fecerunt suis operibus familiares, ut nunc harum argutiarum omnia sint plena.' 'In questo erudito Secolo', says Emanuele Tesauro, who himself received his education from the Society, 'per la bontà degli 'ntelletti, e per la diligente opera della Compagnia di Giesù, il Latino Stile ritornato ci paia di morte à vita.'[3]

After a chapter in which he illustrates copiously the uses to which inscriptions can be put and quotes in full an 'Oratio integra hoc stylo concepta' which he himself delivered in 1677, Weise gives an account of eleven of the principal contemporary practitioners of the art—seven of them Italians, nine of them Jesuits[4]—with specimens of their compositions. His first Book then

---

[1] Quoting passages from Sallust, Tacitus, Pliny, Paterculus and Seneca, and also from Augustine, Jerome and Bernard, which he transposes into lineated epigraphic form. The classical writers, he says (p. 58), 'materiam argutarum Inscriptionum dederunt: Formam ipsam ultimis saeculis reliquerunt.'

[2] 'Et vero postquam e barbarie denuo emergerent literae, atque aliquod antiquitatis esse(t) pretium, in Italia primum Epitaphiis major concessa venustas est, ut, qui talia pangebant, non purae saltem, sed pulchrioris etiam latinitatis relinquere vellent specimen', p. 71.

[3] *Cannochiale Aristotelico* (ed. 1670), p. 239.

[4] They are: Emanuel Thesaurus, Aloysius Juglaris, Johannes Baptista Masculus, Octavius Ferrarius, Leo Matina, Octavius Boldonius, Johannes Palatius, Jacobus Masenius, Bohuslaus Aloysius Balbinus, Nicolaus Avancinus, and Petrus Labbé.

closes with a short and superficial chapter on certain matters of form: the use of capital letters, punctuation, abbreviations, lineation and so on.

In his second Book, which deals with the composition of inscriptions, Weise lays down several rules, of which the two leading ones are these: first, *Nihil scribi debere, nisi quod excitet Lectoris* ADMIRATIONEM; second, *Servandam in omnibus decentem* BREVITATEM. The requirement of Brevity, he goes on to say, does not refer to the length of the inscription as a whole; it means that each thought in it must be concisely expressed, 'ut ubique Lector plura inveniat *cogitanda* quam videt *legenda*'. Hence he lays down the further precept: *Singulas Inscriptionis lineas debere obtinere vim Epigrammatis*—each line of an inscription must of itself have the force of an epigram.[1]

How do you excite *admiratio*? The answer is, by a display of wit—*argutiae, argutezza*—and Weise adopts from one of his eleven practitioners, Jacobus Masenius of Mainz (best known as the author of *Sarcotis*, from which Lauder accused Milton of stealing), the doctrine that there are four *fontes argutiarum*: Repugnantia, Alienatio, Comparatio, and Allusio.

Masenius had developed his analysis of Wit in a treatise called *Familiarum Argutiarum Fontes* (Cologne, 1649), in which he subdivided his 'Fontes' into twenty-two 'venae' (cf. the title-page of a later edition, Plate 49); Weise devotes a chapter to each 'Fons', giving numerous examples of each kind of figure.

EMANUELE TESAURO

The most important person in this phase of the story was undoubtedly Count Emanuele Tesauro, Knight Grand Cross of the Order of SS. Maurice and Lazarus. Tesauro was born at Turin in 1592 and died there in 1675. He was educated by the Jesuits in Milan and became a member of their Society, but left it for the secular priesthood in 1634 and spent the rest of his life in Turin as a historian and epigraphist at the ducal Court of Savoy.

Tesauro was a copious author; his publications (of which there is no satis-factory bibliography) included works on Moral Philosophy (*La Filosofia Morale derivata dall'alto fonte del grande Aristotele Stagirita*, 1670) and History (in particular, a series of accounts of the campaigns in Piedmont, a History of the

---

[1] Weise points out, however, that the French epigraphist, Pierre Labbé (whom he admired beyond all other composers), recognised two types of inscription, in one of which the *line*, in the other the *period*, was the unit of composition. He quotes several examples of Labbé's 'periodic' inscriptions.

49. Title-page of Jacobus Masenius's *Familiarum Argutiarum Fontes* (Cologne, 1688), much enlarged.

IL
CANNOCCHIALE
ARISTOTELICO,

O' ſia, Idéa

DELL'ARGVTA ET INGENIOSA ELOCVTIONE,

Che ſerue à tutta l'Arte

ORATORIA, LAPIDARIA, ET SIMBOLICA.

Esaminata Co' Principii

DEL DIVINO ARISTOTELE,

Dal Conte

D.EMANVELE TESAVRO,

Cavalier Gran Croce De' Santi Mavritio, Et Lazaro.

SECONDA IMPRESSIONE,

Accreſciuta dall' Autore di due nuoui Trattati, cioè,

DE' CONCETTI PREDICABILI, ET DEGLI EMBLEMI.

All'Illuſtriſs:mo, & Eccell:mo Sig.re

LORENZO DELFINO.

IN VENETIA, *Preſſo Paolo Baglioni.* M. DC. LXIII.

Con Licenza de' Superiori, e Priuilegio.

50. Title-page of Emanuele Tesauro's *Cannochiale Aristotelico* (2nd edn, Venice, 1663), enlarged.

Kingdom of Italy under the Barbarians, and several excursions into local history), besides an essay on writing letters in cipher and a number of oratorical and poetical pieces.

The works that concern us are two: a huge critical treatise entitled *Il Cannochiale Aristotelico* and the volume containing his collected Inscriptions.

The *Cannochiale* came out in Venice in 1655, an octavo of 672 pages; it was reprinted nine times (it seems) before the end of the century, always in Italy.[1] It is the richest possible treasure-house for the study of seventeenth-century 'wit'; beside it, Weise's analysis seems amateur and superficial.

Some idea of the contents of this remarkable book may be gathered from its title-page (Plate 50), and from the fact that Tesauro devotes more than two hundred folio pages[2] to analysing the eight different kinds of metaphor that he discovers in Aristotle's *Rhetoric*; he goes on to tell us that the simple inscription, from the tomb of Alexander the Great,

Brevi hac in urna conduntur cineres magni Alexandri,

can be rendered in seventy-seven different witty ways, corresponding to his seventy-seven 'Figure Patetiche', that is, methods of working on the emotions; and he gives an example of each.

The thirteenth chapter of the *Cannochiale* consists of a 'Trattato delle Inscrittioni Argute', in which Tesauro traces the development of lapidary writing. The ancient Romans, he says, composed their inscriptions with plainness and dignity, but without life or point. They had no lapidary style, to be distinguished by the eye or by the ear from their oratorical style. To illustrate this assertion, he takes a passage from Cicero,[3] and shows how he had had to alter it in order to translate it from the oratorical to the lapidary style, which (as he repeatedly reminds us) is half-way between the oratorical and the poetical. He sets out the lapidary version over against the original, and explains the modifications he has had to make in order to reduce Cicero's rotund diction to the concision demanded by the rules of *argutezza*. It will be enough here to quote the opening lines of each version:

[1] This makes it easier to understand why Weise, writing in 1678, had never seen a copy (cf. *De Argutis Inscriptionibus*, ed. 1688, pp. 108, 408). Tesauro, in the dedication prefixed by him to the fifth (1670) edition of the *Cannochiale*, speaks of the book as having been printed 'da diverse Stampe Italiane e straniere'; I have not come across any 'foreign' edition.

[2] My references are to the fifth edition (Turin, 1670), pp. 266–481.   [3] *Phil.* XIV, xii.

O fortunata Mors, quae Naturae debita, pro Patria est potissimum reddita. Vos vero Patriae natos iudico, quorum etiam nomen a Marte est: ut idem Deus Urbem hanc gentibus; vos huic Urbi genuisse videatur. In fuga foeda Mors est: in Victoria gloriosa. Etenim Mars ipse ex acie fortissimum quemque pignerari solet. Illi igitur impii quos cecidistis, etiam ad Inferos poenas Parricidii luent: vos vero qui extremum spiritum in Victoria effudistis, Piorum estis sedem, et locum consecuti.

'Ben tu vedi', observes Tesauro, 'in questo Elogio una bella forma *Oratoria* da rotolar dal pergamo; ma non già *Lapidaria* da intagliare in un Marmo. Ben vedi ciascuna Periodo Concettosa, ma non Concia: e li Concetti per lo più fabricati sù la Metafora, non molto acuta: e sù l'Opposito, non molto ristretto; mancandovi il Laconismo, che mal si accorda con la ritondità Periodica.' He then reduces it 'alla maniera Lapidaria' as follows:

Fortunata Mors,

Naturae debita; Patriae reddita.

Legio vere Martia,

A Patrio Numine Nomen adepta.

Vt idem Armorum Deus

Vrbem hanc Gentibus: vos huic Vrbi genuerit.

In fuga, foeda Mors; in Victoria, gloriosa.

Mars enim fortisimos pigneratur.

Vos victi victores,

Pii impios occidistis, occisi.

Itaque, dum impios mulctant Inferi;

Vos Superas inter sedes, triumphatis.

'Non vedi tu', Tesauro asks triumphantly, 'con quanto piccol mutamento, un'Elogio *ascoltabile* sia divenuto *leggibile*?' 'La maniera Tulliana', he declares, is excellent for the ear, but the other is better for the reader's eye. He then turns to Tacitus, and displays a passage[1] which, he says, can be set out in lapidary form simply by appropriate lineation, 'senza mutare una sillaba':

[1] *Hist.* I, xlix.

Hunc exitum habuit Sergius Galba:
Tribus et septuaginta Annis, quinque Principes emensus.
Alieno Imperio felicior, quam suo.
Illi vetus nobilitas, magnae opes, medium ingenium.
Magis extra vitia, quam cum virtutibus.
Famae nec incuriosus, nec venditator.
Pecuniae alienae non appetens, suae parcus, publicae avarus.
Amicorum, Libertorumque,
Ubi in bonos incidisset, sine reprehensione patiens:
Ubi in malos, usque ad culpam ignarus.

Compare this *elogium* with Cicero's, and you will have plenty to think about, says Tesauro, concerning 'la differenza dallo stile *Oratorio*, al *Lapidario*'.

It was the Tacitean style, Tesauro tells us, that he adopted when, being little more than a boy, he had to devise a form of *elogium* for his *Caesares*,[1] and it was the success of his *Caesares* that set him off on his career as composer and connoisseur of inscriptions. That was in 1619, the year in which Ferdinand II was elected Emperor. The election had caused great rejoicing in Catholic countries: the Universities rang with the declamations of panegyrists and their walls were covered with *elogia*. Tesauro's contribution, in Milan, was a series of inscriptions of about twenty lines apiece, each of them devoted to one of the first twelve Caesars, in the highly pointed, witty, style that was to set the fashion for the rest of the century. They must have been posted up on paper or parchment; it was not until much later that they were reduced to print.[2]

In the following year, 1620, Pope Paul V decreed the Beatification of Francis Xavier. Tesauro's contribution to the celebrations of this event in Milan took the form of eleven inscriptions describing scenes from Xavier's life, in the lapidary style he did so much to popularise. 'Quod genus laudationis', says Tesauro's editor Panealbi, 'ea tempestate maxime novum', excited such admiration that when, two years later, under Gregory XV, Blessed Francis Xavier was canonised, 'haec ipsa Elogia in publico viarum apparatu Neapoli

---

[1] 'Quanto à me', he says (*Cannochiale*, p. 599), 'io mi appigliai à questo secondo stile per gli Eloggi de' Cesari, come più legibile. Benche, sicome allora io era un Garzoncello; non è maraviglia, se lo stile sia giovenile; più vivace che sodo.'

[2] At any rate in the form of a book; the earliest known edition of the *Caesares* appeared under Tesauro's name at Lyons in 1635. Two years later, an edition was published in Oxford in duodecimo; this little book is of special interest because it contains a set of Latin verses by George Herbert.

exposita fuerint et mira ingeniorum aviditate perlecta, atque transcripta'. They were not printed, however, until the collected edition of Tesauro's inscriptions appeared forty years later.

In 1621, the year after Xavier's Beatification, occurred an event that was celebrated with solemnities throughout the Catholic world: the death of Philip III. In Milan, the 'literary' side of the whole business—'Regii Funeris apparatus universus, quoad rem literariam'—was entrusted to Tesauro, whose work (according to Panealbi) was 'ab omnibus facile agnoscendum'.

A huge inscription was displayed, between two figures of Death, outside the Cathedral; inside, at the four corners of the catafalque, were four more inscriptions, testifying to the grief of Philip's successor, of the Regent, of the city of Milan, and of the whole world. Daylight was excluded from the interior of the cathedral, which was brilliantly lit with branching candelabra, and the twelve spaces between the columns of the nave were filled with figures representing the Provinces of the King's domains, each commemorating, 'arguta Inscriptione', one of the virtues of the deceased monarch. Each of the tablets carried, besides the inscription, two verse epigrams and a 'symbolum' consisting of an emblem and a motto.

During the next ten years, Tesauro consolidated his reputation in Turin as an epigraphist. In July 1630, on the death of Carlo Emanuele I, his successor Amedeo called on Tesauro and his brother Lodovico to plan the ceremonial removal of his father's body from its temporary resting-place at Savogliana and its interment at Monreale: Lodovico was to make a funeral oration, Emanuele was entrusted with 'universi apparatus dispositionem'. Amedeo's short reign was so distracted that the funeral solemnities were never celebrated, but Panealbi says that the manuscripts of the intended inscriptions, and a 'delineatio' of the whole *apparatus*, were placed in his hands (presumably by the composer, who was still alive) and he included them in the collection of Tesauro's inscriptions that he published in 1666. They illustrate the whole of the Duke's reign, and are even more numerous and elaborate than those exhibited for the funeral *apparatus* of Philip III.

In February 1631, an heir was born to Philip IV, the Don Baltasar familiar to us from the canvases of Velasquez; in Milan, the Senate decreed a service of thanksgiving and a display of fireworks, and entrusted to the 'ingenium' of Tesauro 'utriusque apparatus literariam operam'.

Since military virtues are the chief glory of a prince, Tesauro thought it appropriate to devise for these celebrations a sort of pageant representing Vulcan forging for Thetis the armour of her infant son Achilles. A representation of Mount Etna was erected in the middle of the *piazza*, with an inscription on each of its four sides; the whole *piazza* was enclosed with porticoes, like the Circus Maximus, and four more inscriptions adorned the columns of the two gateways that gave ingress: these were 'festiviore, ac proinde licentiore, stylo animatas'; Tesauro sets them out, with evident self-satisfaction, in the *Cannochiale*.[1] Here is one of them:

HOSPES QVAM SPECTAS MOLEM

PENSILIBVS FLORENTEM FLAMMIS

NOVA EST ÆTNA

CLARANDIS REGVM NATALIBVS NATA

MIRARIS AVSTRIAE FORTVNAE NOVOS NASCI MONTES

CVI NOVI NASCVNTVR MVNDI?

PLVS EST OPTIMVM REGEM NASCI QVAM MONTEM

MAIVS QVIDDAM MIRABERE

NAM SVIS IGNIBVS INTERITVRA NASCITVR ÆTNA

EADEM SIBI PYRA ERIT ET PYRAVSTA

NEC TAMEN DOLET

QVIPPE LAETITIA FLAMMIS IMMORI NON EST MORI

FRIGIDA IPSA BRVMA

IN ROGALI FLAMMA REGALEM ARDOREM SENTIT

DENIQVE ORBIS VNIVERSVS

DVLCES IN FLAMMAS LIQVESCERET

NISI REGNATVRO VIVERE IVBERETVR

APAGE INVIDE

HANC AD FLAMMAM NI CALES

ADAMAS ES NON ADAMANS

[1] Ed. 1670, pp. 603–6.

This, with its Hyperboles ('novi nascuntur Mundi'), its 'Oppositiones' ('suis ignibus interitura Aetna'), its 'Metaphorae Proportionis' ('Eadem sibi Pyra et Pyrausta'), its 'Hypotyposes' ('florentem Flammis') and its 'Aequivocationes' ('Adamas, non Adamans') may serve as a type of Tesauro's 'Inscrittioni Argute'.[1]

Eleven more inscriptions adorned the arches of the *piazza* (these were so concise, however, as to be little more than mottoes),[2] and around its circumference were stationed figures representing the Kingdoms and Provinces subject to Spanish rule, each holding aloft a torch which lit up the night until, at a given signal, Etna erupted, there was a loud report, and the whole 'Circus', 'vario laetoque lusu', went up in flames.

It is not surprising that when an heir was born to the House of Savoy in September 1632, and Turin resolved to celebrate the event in the usual fashion with a service of thanksgiving and a display of fireworks, Tesauro should have been called upon to devise the pageant and to write the inscriptions for it.

The prince's name being Giacinto, the whole affair was floral: a huge triumphal arch was erected against the façade of the Cathedral, and over it, as if descending from heaven, was the figure of a Celestial Genius, carrying, in a golden basket, shaped like a cradle, a hyacinth of cerulean blue with the Virgilian legend *blandos fundens cunabula flores*. Tesauro's inscription on the arch, and all the decorations, elaborated this floral theme: woodland nymphs played the part of caryatids, and figures of Spring and Flora, garlanded with hyacinths, scattered flowers, while four shields adorning the capitals of the columns illustrated (with classical mottoes) those virtues of the hyacinth that were attributable to the young prince.

So much for the 'religious' part of the celebrations.

The theme of the firework display was the Zodiac; in the principal square was erected an amphitheatre like a zodiacal circle, 'eleganter columnatus

---

[1] It is quoted by Ottavio Boldoni (*Epigraphica*, 1660, p. 9), who was present at the festivities, as a 'luculentum exemplum' of a *temporary* inscription—an exception to the rule that inscriptions are designed to endure as long as possible. This, says Boldoni, 'nata erat incendio, non ergo diuturnitati', and was therefore inscribed not on stone but on wood; it was only by good fortune, he adds, that it was preserved as an example of the work of its composer, 'artis Magistro consummatissimo, et plurimis id genus publicatis argumentis perceleberrimo'.

[2] The motto, often displayed heraldically, was of course ubiquitous throughout the sixteenth and seventeenth centuries; but, consisting as it did of no more than a phrase, it afforded no scope for effective lineation and plays no part in the development of the inscription as a literary form.

ornatusque'. Round it stood statues representing eleven signs of the Zodiac, and in the midst, raised on high, reclining on a throne composed of silver clouds, was the twelfth sign, Taurus, the eponymous symbol of the city of Turin, the birthplace of the new prince. He was being crowned by Jupiter, and round him were seated the Pleiades and figures representing the rivers of Turin, each pouring flames, instead of water, from her urn. Every one of the attendant Zodiacal signs was furnished with an appropriate motto, and Tesauro provided Taurus with an inscription which was 'flammigerae totius celebritatis Argumentum':

NOVVM ASTRVM

POST LVCIFVGAS TEMPESTATES

IN AVGVSTO TAVRI SINV REPENTE NATVM

ASTRA OMNIA

FELICIORIS AEVI PRINCIPIVM OMINATA

FESTIVIS LAMPADVM LVDIS GRATVLANTVR

As the climax of the nocturnal display, when all the Zodiacal signs were shining brightly, a ball of fire, symbolising the royal infant, was to be precipitated from the dark sky into the bosom of Taurus, like the new star that proverbially heralded a new and happier age. At this, the other signs were to discharge successively the fireworks they were holding, as in a torch-race; 'tum toto Theatro, Cylindri, Faces, Bolides, atque infinita flammarum ingenia, convolarent. Denique Taurus ipse, hilares in flammas abiret; totumque Solium atque Theatrum ingenti sonitu, variisque ignium lusibus conflagraret.'

Unfortunately, says the chronicler, 'temporis angustiae' prevented this effective climax from being enacted.

For forty years more Tesauro provided the Court of Savoy with inscriptions for celebrations of births, deaths, marriages, and visits of important persons; at the reception, for instance, of Queen Christina of Sweden, who passed through Turin in 1655, he devised an *apparatus* of which the centre-piece was a Phoenix, with appropriate inscriptions.

In 1666, ten years before he died, there appeared an official collection of Tesauro's *Inscriptiones*, edited by his friend Emanuele Filiberto Panealbi, Professor of Roman Law in the University of Turin. It had been anticipated by at least one unauthorised collection (Venice, 1654), and it was itself many times reprinted—editions were produced as far afield as Frankfurt and Leipzig

(1688). This book no doubt answered a demand. Tesauro's new lapidary style was popular, and the publication of his collected inscriptions increased that popularity and spread it far and wide.

The folio edition of Tesauro's *Inscriptiones* published in 1670 provides, in its engraved title-page, an interesting example of pictorial history (Plate 51). The interpretation of the scene seems to be obvious: the Lapidary Muse, it would appear, is inscribing a text on stone at the dictation of Mercury, the Messenger of the Gods.

A closer look tells a different story: the Muse, in fact, is not taking down a text from dictation: she has completed it, and is merely deepening the letters. And the book to which Mercury is calling her attention is a blank book—what look like lines of text are in fact lines of shading. 'No,' he is saying, 'not *there*, upon the stone, but *here*, upon paper, is the proper place for the effusions of the epigraphic Muse'—the engraving is, in fact, a pictorial record of the transformation of the lapidary inscription into the text of a printed book—its migration from stone to paper.

The contents of the collection explain and justify its frontispiece: it is divided almost equally into: (1) inscriptions that are lapidary in the literal sense—*Rerum, Locorumque Inscriptiones et Monumenta* (including Tesauro's grandiose epitaph on the gigantic monument erected in 1666 to the Doge Giovanni Pesaro in the Frari in Venice) and *Regiarum Aedium Ornamenta* (his inscriptions still adorn the walls of the Royal Palace at Turin and the Stupinigi hunting-lodge); (2) 'temporary' inscriptions for great occasions, such as those described above: *Funebres Apparatus, Natalitiae Pompae, Sacrae Celebritates*, and *Publicae Principum Receptiones*; and (3) *Inscriptiones Historicae, Id est, Patriarcharum Genealogia*. This last, cryptically named, section was a novelty, for it contained inscriptions intended solely for print. The sections I have numbered (1) and (2) contain the printed texts of inscriptions that had been composed for public display, either permanently on stone or temporarily on the wooden panels of some *machina temporaria*; but the *Inscriptiones Historicae* were never intended to appear anywhere except upon the pages of a printed book.

The editor explains, in a foreword to the *Patriarchae*, how its contents came into being. The Duke Carlo Emanuele I, having embarked on a treatise *De Regnorum Exordiis*, in which he proposed to trace the history of monarchy 'a Protoparente Adamo, ad sua usque Tempora', asked Tesauro for a series of

51. Title-page of Emanuele Tesauro's *Inscriptiones* (Turin, 1670).

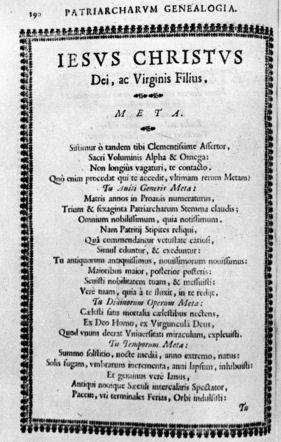

IESVS CHRISTVS

Dei, ac Virginis Filius.

M E T A.

Siſtimur ò tandem tibi Clementiſsime Aſſertor,
Sacri Voluminis Alpha & Omega:
Non longiùs vagaturi, te contacto.
Quò enim procedat qui te accedit, vltimam rerum Metam?
Tu Aniſi Generis Meta:
Matris annos in Proauis numeraturus,
Trium & ſexaginta Patriarcharum Stemma claudis;
Omnium nobiliſſimum, quia notiſſimum.
Nam Patritij Stipites reliqui,
Quà commendantur vetuſtate carioſi,
Simul eduntur, & exeduntur:
Tu antiquorum antiquiſſimus, nouiſſimorum nouiſſimus:
Maioribus maior, poſterior poſteris:
Sciuiſti nobilitatem tuam, & meſſuiſti:
Verè tuam, quia à te fluxit, in te redijt.
Tu Diuinorum Operum Meta:
Cæleſti ſatu mortalia cæleſtibus nectens,
Ex Deo Homo, ex Virgunculâ Deus,
Quod vnum deerat Vniuerſitati miraculum, expleuiſti.
Tu Temporum Meta:
Summo ſolſtitio, nocte mediâ, anno extremo, natus:
Solis fugam, vmbrarum incrementa, anni lapſum, inhibuiſti:
Et geminus verè Ianus,
Antiqui nouique Sæculi intercalaris Spectator,
Pacem, vti terminales Ferias, Orbi indulſiſti:

Tu

Tu Dignitatum Meta:
Quâ in Stabulo contactâ, Purpurati Aſtronomi retroceſsére.
Nam quis vltra Bubile illud faſtus explicet,
Vbi ſuperbiæ frænum eſt fœnum?
O nouæ Aſtronomiæ ſectanei Reges!
Cæteri Præſepe inter Stellas, hi Stellas in Præſepi obſeruarunt.
Scitè igitur capitum décora tuos ante pedes proiecére:
Gnari, dignitates deſinere vbi incipiunt.
Tu Moſaica Legis Meta:
Duriſſima iura circumciſus circumcidiſti,
Et inamœna Synagogæ ſpatia metaſti;
Lapideo illo gladio pro limitaneo lapide, infixo.
Tu Sapientia Meta:
Phariſaicam Templi Exedram duodennis euertiſti.
Nam te audito, qui omnia docebant, nihil ſe ſcire didicerunt:
Et Infante Magiſtro, ſe nouerunt Infantes.
Tu Inferna potentia Meta:
Spectante Solitudine cum Lucifero congreſſus,
Auidum eſuriendo ſtrangulaſti;
Et inceſtam illam naturam, æternæ flammæ cuſtodem,
Malarum Veſtalium ſupplicio, de rupe impellens,
Heſperum feciſti ex Lucifero.
Tu Peccati Meta:
Iordanem intrando abluens, vt aliorum ſordes elueres,
Herculeæ inſtar columnæ, fluctibus demerſus,
Vndarum & ſcelerum curſum progredi vetuiſti.
Tu Votorum Meta:
Patrium orbem benemerendo diſcurrens,
Fatigato ſæpiùs pede, numquam manu,
Supplicia à ſupplicibus auertiſti.
Tu Mortis Meta:
Arboris eiuſdem paxillo, quo Mors Adamum transfixerat,
Æquâ talione Mortem confixiſti:
Quæ funeſtiſſimo exacto ſtadio,

Ad

52. Emanuele Tesauro's *Inscriptiones*, pp. 190–1.

elogia of the Patriarchs and the Popes, 'Authoris nostri Lapidario stylo lucubrata', to be interspersed and lighten the bulk of what he feared might be too heavy a composition. Carlo Emanuele never published his treatise, and when he died in 1630, Tesauro, who had not completed the series of Patriarchs, put the work aside. He continued it, however, at the request of the Duke's successor, and completed it in 1643. He never attempted the Popes—thus disappointing, according to Panealbi, much eager expectation.[1]

The *Patriarchae* consists of 150 *elogia*, varying from fifty to a hundred lines apiece, and constituting a body of almost 10,000 lines of lapidary writing. It embraces a complete genealogy of the descent of Jesus Christ from Adam, including a number of his collateral human relations; Plate 52 gives an idea of what its text is like.

[1] Tesauro's failure may be thought to have been redeemed by *Sacrum Triregnum Seu Singulorum Pontificum Praeclariora Gesta Elogiis, Poesique Descripta*, which contains a series of 'lapidary' *elogia* of all the Popes, by Iacopo Ciampalantes, dedicated to Pope Clement IX, Venice, 1669.

The influence of this work was felt all over Europe, and it seems to have been circulated widely in manuscript as well as in print. Panealbi declared that the text he printed in 1666 in his edition of the collected Inscriptions was taken from an autograph corrected by the author; the earliest printed edition that I can trace[1]—which was published at Milan in 1645, and is dedicated to the Cardinal Archbishop, Monti, to welcome him back in 1644 from the conclave at which Innocent X was elected—is said by the printer to be based on a MS found in Rome.[2] Since the work was only finished two years before, viz. (as the text of its last *elogium* declares), in 1643, it must have been circulated in MS as soon as its text was completed, if not before. It immediately became very popular; in 1651 a translation into hexameters appeared in Antwerp, and in the same year the original text was republished in London. It was included in the unauthorised collection of Tesauro's Inscriptions that came out in Venice in 1654, and in another collection published at Genoa in 1655; in 1657 another (separate) edition appeared in London, and another in Rouen in 1667. In 1669 the *Patriarchae* was reprinted at Mainz together with another book of *elogia*, the *Christus Jesus* of Aloysius Juglar.[3]

THE SPREAD OF THE LAPIDARY BOOK

Juglar, like Tesauro, was a Jesuit at the court of Turin, and rivalled him in designing festal displays for the Duke and composing inscriptions for them; he was responsible for the funeral *apparatus* for Vittorio Amedeo in 1637 (Plate 47). He seems to have stolen Tesauro's thunder with his *Christus Jesus*, in which he tells the gospel story, scene by scene, in a series of 100 *elogia*, each about 50 lines long.

Juglar's book came out in 1641 (before Tesauro's *Patriarchae* was completed, let alone printed), and its contents were many times reprinted, sometimes, like Tesauro's, with the rest of their author's miscellaneous inscriptions. In his

[1] Itself a 're-impression', according to the wording of the Licence: 'Re-imprimatur'.
[2] 'Perierat hoc ipsum volumen, amisso ante aliquot annos per frequentes legentium manus autographo: nisi exemplar unum, quod aliquis Romae de autographo surripuerat, emersisset.'
[3] The authority accorded to the *Patriarchae* may be judged from Menestrier, *op. cit.* pp. 268–70: 'Enfin pour voir de combien de manieres ces Inscriptions se peuvent tourner, il ne faut que jetter les yeux sur les Eloges des Patriarches de l'ancien Testament de L'Abbé Tesoro'; Menestrier names 85 'figures' and continues: 'Ces quatre-vingt et cinq sortes d'Eloges et d'Inscriptions peuvent servir de modele pour en faire de semblables; et comme ce livre du Comte Tesoro est commun, ayant esté imprimé plus de sept ou huit fois en diverses formes, je ne m'arresteray pas à en donner des exemples.'

address to the reader, Juglar has some shrewd things to say about this style of composition: 'Genus hoc scriptionis iam nosti', he declares, 'nostro, seu natum seu renatum in saeculo, pleraque nobilitavit ingenia.' Its readers must not look for 'periodi', or swelling Ciceronian cadences, nor for purity of Latin: 'Acutus videri qui vult, saepe Latinus esse non potest.' Take it, he counsels, in small pieces: 'Cave ne opsonium hoc, panem putes. Genus hoc cibi, excitandis ingeniis natum est, non pascendis.' Then, changing his metaphor, 'Flores hi sunt, carpuntur per se singuli summis digitis, non tota immissa falce metuntur. Ubi unum, aut alterum delibatis Elogium, ne fastidire alia debeas, novam famem expecta.'

Juglar was not the first Jesuit composer to publish a book of paper inscriptions; the earliest example of this kind of book which I have discovered is a collection of *elogia* of twelve of the Fathers of the Church, *Vitae ac Elogia XII Patrum*, written by Giovanni Andrea Alberti, S.J., and published at Turin in 1638.

Alberti's book consists of more than 5,000 lines of inscriptional biography—a more extended effort in this line, it seems, than anything that had hitherto appeared. In his preface, addressed *Anonymo Rhetori*, he expresses misgivings lest the lapidary style should seem unsuited to such a lengthy undertaking. 'Insolens opinor ipsa tibi scriptura videbitur, dum ad singulos quosque versus concidit, ritu carminum'; but if you treat each episode, he suggests, as a separate *elogium*, all will be well: 'atqui, ut in brevibus elogiis, nemo est quin ignoscat, quidni etiam hic? ubi elogia tot habere te credito, quot gesta narrata'. He is well aware, he says, how sparingly one should indulge in this 'nova licentia', 'qua depravari, atque corrumpi ingenuam eloquentiam plerique aiunt'.

As Alberti himself was evidently aware, the new epigraphy was not without its critics. Foremost among these was Ottavio Boldoni,[1] whose *Epigraphica*, a huge treatise on the composition of inscriptions of all kinds, came out in

---

[1] B. 1595, d. 1680; Bishop of Teano. Boldoni had two distinguished brothers, Sigismondo, a Professor at Pavia, who was cut off by the plague in 1630 at the age of 33, and Giovanni-Niccolò, author of several works of piety, who died in 1670. Ottavio commemorated both of them in *elogia* contained in a collection of his own inscriptions: *Epigraphae Religiosae Memoriales Mortuales Encomiasticae* (Rome, 1670) (see my article on a MS of Sigismondo's *Amores*, *The Library*, XVII, no. 4, December 1962, pp. 308–11).

1660 (Plate 53).[1] Boldoni's name for the inscription is *elogium*, a word he uses as practically the equivalent of *epigraphē*. He carefully distinguishes *elogium* in his sense from the literary type of *elogium* made familiar by Paolo Giovio and writers like him—'Historiae et Orationes titulo praefixae elogii'. Such historical and oratorical performances, he says, 'nihil commune habent nobiscum'. No more have extravagant panegyrics of broadsheet proportions, 'prolixae lucubrationes, quae macrocolla inferciunt', of which he cites dozens of examples. While he was compiling his list of such monstrosities, he came (he tells us) upon a supreme example of them—the *Vitae ac Elogia XII Patrum* of Alberti, whom he calls 'summus Elogiasta nostri temporis'. Alberti's lengthy lapidary biographies, according to Boldoni, are far too prolix to qualify as *elogia* in his sense of the term. They are examples of a newly fashionable type of *elogium*, the excessively long 'lucubratio' made up of lines that are themselves too short: 'Irrepsit [he says] quippe hodie in mentes plurimorum idea illa dicendi, veteribus ignorata, rationi absurdissima, ut longum quemque ad molem magni voluminis sermonem in genere quolibet vel disputativo et contentioso, non nisi ad cultum laconicum componant, abrupte admodum, presse, minutim, concisis numeris, repetitis spiritibus.'

The composers of such productions, he says, have rightly been called 'asthmatici'; 'anhelant, non loquuntur'; their efforts exhaust the patience of those who hear or read them. 'Supersedemus exemplis', he concludes, 'ne cui infensi simus: Satis enim ostendunt moniti nostri momentum, quae quotidie prodeunt monstra huius generis'—a plain reference to the performances of Tesauro and his followers.

The first five of Boldoni's six books are devoted to the qualities proper to the true *elogium*—'Perspicuitas', 'Brevitas', and so on; they are illustrated with over fifteen hundred examples of inscriptions, ancient and modern, the ancient being drawn mainly from Gruter, the modern from the collections of Sweerts. It is only in his last book that he turns to *inscriptiones argutae*. In his 'Prolusio' to this Book he explains that he had had it in mind to pass over this branch of his subject very briefly, 'ne nos forte coeptis illorum infaustis videremur

---

[1] At Perugia, 'Ex Typographia Camerali, et Episcopali'. Between the date of the original approval of publication by the Barnabite Order (April 1656) and the final Imprimatur (November 1657), Boldoni had been appointed to his Bishopric. The full title of his book, which runs to over 800 pages, is *Epigraphica sive Elogia Inscriptionesque quoduis genus pangendi ratio Ubi de inscribendis Tabulis, Symbolis, Clypeis, Trophaeis, Donariis, Obeliscis, Aris, Tumulis, Musaeis, Hortis, Villis, Fontibus, et si qua sunt alia huiusmodi Monumenta, facili methodo dissertatur.*

EPIGRAPHICA

SIVE

ELOGIA INSCRIPTIONESQVE

Quoduis genus pangendi ratio

VBI

DE INSCRIBENDIS

Tabulis,Symbolis,Clypeis,Trophaeis,
Donarijs,Obeliscis,Aris,Tumulis,
Musaeis,Hortis,Villis,Fontibus,

Et si qua sunt alia huiusmodi Monumenta, facili methodo dissertatur

Subiectisque Exemplis Antiquis, ac Recentibus

Nonnullis etiam ex vtrisque nondum vulgatis Praecepta dilucidantur.

Auctore

OCTAVIO BOLDONIO MEDIOLANENSI
ex Clericis Regularibus Barnabitis Ordinis S. Pauli,
Episcopo Theanensi.

AD SERENISSIMVM
COSMVM MEDICEVM
ETRVRIAE PRINCIPEM·

AVGVSTAE PERVSIAE · MDCLX·
Ex Typographia Camerali , & Episcopali, Apud Bartolos , & Angelum Laurentium.
DE LICENTIA PRAESIDVM.

53. Title-page of Ottavio Boldoni's *Epigraphica* (Perugia, 1660).

applaudere, atque ultro in praeceps labentibus insistere amplius subiectis stimulis, ubi fraena nulla sint satis.' The fashion for such writing is so rife, he says, that what is needed is not so much 'praeceptores, qui Argutiarum inueniendarum edoceant modum; quam censores, qui modum praescribant inuentis'. 'Princeps amoenitatis literariae, Emanuel Thesaurus', he says, has anticipated him 'opere nimirum illo admirando, et (ut is ad Amicos) quadragesimum in annum presso', the *Canocchiale Aristotelico*. It is his task, never attempted by Tesauro, to discover the kinds of *argutia* appropriate to the *elogium* by considering the kindred case of the *epigramma*. His conclusion is summed up in a series of 'monita', the effect of which is that wit must not be over-elaborated: 'Arte summa hebetari Argutias, ac perdi', and that the passion to be witty at all costs 'sanis mentibus postremum esse, insanis primum'. The elaborate analysis of the nature of wit contained in his sixth Book is supported by over a hundred examples of 'witty' inscriptions; but the main purpose of his treatise was to serve as an antidote to the craving for wit in epigraphy, and it may stand to present-day readers as a reminder of the fact that the classical strain of epigraphy, though it lost its original purity, never quite dried up: Boldoni's *Epigraphica* does for the conventional inscription what Tesauro's *Canocchiale* does for the *inscriptio arguta*.[1]

By the middle of the seventeenth century, then, the lapidary style had ceased to be a 'nova licentia' and had become a recognised literary *genre*, and the printed book consisting of *elogia* written simply for publication in print was a common phenomenon, especially in the north of Italy. It had been invented by the Jesuits and was used by them mainly as an instrument of piety; they strung together Lives of the Popes, of the Patriarchs, of the Saints, of the Founder of Christianity, all consisting of *elogia* in lapidary form.

The *genre* was to undergo one further and final development. It crossed the

---

[1] 'Pour se former à ce genre d'écrire', says Menestrier (*op. cit.* p. 235), 'il seroit bon de lire le *Canocchiale Aristotelico* de l'Abbé Tesoro, qui traite à fond des Inscriptions, et le Volume que Bolducius [*sic*] a fait sur ce même sujet, *de Arte Epigraphica*.' 'Ceux qui voudront imiter [les Inscriptions antiques]', Menestrier continues, 'en forme d'Eloges, replies de pointes, de pensées delicates, d'allusions, et de sentences d'un style serré et coupé, doivent lire les Cesars et les Patriarches de L'Abbé Tesoro: *Christi hominis Dei Elogia*, *Virtutes Infulatae*, et les autres Eloges du Pere Juglaris. *Elogia Sacra*...du Pere Labbé, les Eloges des douze Fondateurs Religieux du Pere Alberti. Les Eloges du P. Masculus, et les Inscriptions du P. Vrsus.' 'Il est vray', he concludes, 'que tout le monde ne s'accommode par de ces pointes et de cette prose coupée, qui est plus du goust des Italiens que du nostre. Neanmoins en ces Decorations elles se peuvent souffrir, pourvû que les Inscriptions ne soient pas longues.'

ΣΙΔΗΡΕΟΥ τῶ ΠΑΤΡΟΣ,
ΕΙΡΗΝΙΚΟΣ ὁ ΥΙΟΣ,
ΤΗΒΕΝΝΗ ἰσοδύναμ〉. ΣΑΓΟΝ ἐγείρει.
Ἐκ τῶ ΛΕΟΝΤΟΣ γεννηθεὶς ὁ ΑΜΝΟΣ,
ὁ ἐκ τῶ ΕΡΝΕΣΤΟΥ ΦΡΙΔΕΡΕΙΚΟΣ.
Αἰνίγμα ἀληθὲς Σαμψωνικὸν·
ΕΚ ΤΟΥ ΕΣΘΟΝΤΟΣ ΕΞΗΛΘΕΝ ΒΡΩΣΙΣ,
ΚΑΙ ΕΞ ΙΣΧΥΡΟΥ ΕΞΗΛΘΕΝ ΓΛΥΚΥ.
Πρῶτ〉 μιξϑεὶς τῶν Αὐστριακῶν Καισάρων πολυμήτωρ
ΣΕΒΑΣΤΟΣ.
τὸν τῶ λαῶ τόπον πληρώσας.
ἢ τῶ ΕΙΡΗΝΙΚΟΥ δῶμα ἀπήνεγκεν
πάντων ἀρχὴ γενέσις· ἐπεὶ ἡ
ΑΡΧΩΝ ΤΗΣ ΕΙΡΗΝΗΣ.
ἐπὶ μίαν τῆς τῆς ΕΙΡΗΝΗΣ ϑησαυρῷ
ΜΕΓΙΣΤΟΣ ΑΥΤΟΚΡΑΤΩΡ.
ἐν ᾧντι αὐτὸς ὁ Θεὸς ἐστὶ ἐπέγραψε.
πρὸς ἄλλων ἐξαίνει.
ὃς ἱερομύημις ἐσέξαμι πολύτεκν〉.
ΕΚ ΤΗΣ ΠΟΛΕΩΣ ΤΗΣ ΕΙΡΗΝΗΣ, οἷα ἀπ᾽ ἀναρίθμων ἐκλέκτ〉,
ὁ ΕΙΡΗΝΙΚΟΣ.
Εὐσέβει
ἐν ἱερῷ τῆς Ψ ἱλασμῶ ἕρπει, τὸν τὸν Εγείρει ἱλασμὸν ἀπηλθέι,
ἰλὰφ· ἱλάσκεται τὸν ἔρχεται
ΦΡΙΔΕΡΕΙΚΟΣ
Εἰρήνης τῶ ΦΙΛΗΜΑΤΙ ἁγίαν τὸν ΓΗΝ ΕΚΤΣΑΣ
ΑΥΣΤΡΙΑΚΟΣ ὄντ〉 ὁ ΒΡΟΥΤΟΣ τᾶς βασιλείας ὑπερήντι,
ᾧτι ἐν ᾧ αὐτὸν τῆ ΧΡΣΤΙΑν, ἐπὶ τῆ ΕΛΑΙΑ
στατὸν ἐδήσαντι
πλουβαίαν
ὁ μὲν τῶ ΣΑΓΟΥ μιμεὶας· τὸς δῆ ΤΑΒΕΝΝΗΣ ἰσογενὴς
τὸν Ἀρχὴν καθεργασθεὶς ἐν ΕΛΑΙΑ, ἰσχύει ἐν ΕΙΡΗΝΗ.

Vix Adolescens FRIDERICVS,
Iam Christi vestigia secutus non æquis passibus, ièd æquis.
Nam *Viri* viam in *Adolescentiâ* signavit.
A Matre Hierosolymam abijt: sed quia rediturus non valedixit
Hierosolymam abijt: pacificus ad visionem pacis.
Credo, quò propius & promptius pacem disceret, illuc abijt;
Nam pax vix discitur, nisi videatur.
Rex futurus orbis illuc abire planè debuit,
Vbi rex Regũ, hoc est, primum exemplar imperantũm, seu Autographũ
vel impressum, vel expressum,
Et quò clarius pateret in nocte editum est,
Gnarâ Divinitate.
Quòd & lux nimia instar tenebrarum excæcet,& Majestas nimia invidos
faciat:
Inter quæ invidia tanto pejor est;
Quòd inter duos,vel non diu, vel non tutò liceat imperare.
Terram

Terram denique accessit: sed Hierosolymæ juvenis quidem, at regius
discipulus,
Tracturus inde præcepta, ubi ille, qui non potuit non imperare, voluit
ministrare.
Applaudat ei lingua sacra,
Qui terram sacram Austrio pede est veneratus.

פרידריבש ר שלמה:
חית שנים של — אידגישתהו
תחביר בשלום שורך
ראשון לביאן עטרך
נשא במיים אידכתירך:

Redux Hierosolymâ loco miraculorum FRIDERICVS,
Vnum, sed miraculorum omnium maximum tulit miraculum,
Quòd ad Imperium rogari debuit.
Erravi.
Majus miraculum est, quod precibus concesserit.
Nam in Portis Hierosolymitanis & legit, & didicit,
Eadem vidi iter ad crucem porrigi, quà ad triumphos.
Quanquam & hoc vel maximè mirer:
Quòd quisquam FRIDERICVM rogaverit, ut imperaret:
Nisi fortassis hæc Austriacorum vel felicitas, vel virtus sit,
Vt, ubi de Rege eligendo quæritur,
Cedentibus alijs, illi ad Imperia rogari debeant,
Id est:
Vt dignentur prodesse, quòd soli sciunt, & tantùm non soli possunt:
Anno M. CD. XL. mortuo paulò ante Alberto Secundo,
Francofurti Rex Romanorum declaratur,
Filio Mirabilium mundi succedente: miraculo hoc mirabilius,
Quòd in pace miles sic præliaretur,
Tanquam hostis nemo obstreperet, ubique pacifico,
Novo pugnandi genere pro gladio oleam circumegit.
Dignus FRIDERICVS, dici
Cui, quidquid alijs rixa & bellum est, Pax fuit:
Ipso etiam Marte stupente, aut si quod cruentum magis ingenium est,
Aliquem inveriri potuisse,
I   Qui

54. Pages from *Coronae Duodecim Caesarum* (Vienna, 1654).

Alps, and was employed as an instrument not of piety but of political controversy.[1] The *elogium* was a convenient form in which to panegyrise not only individuals but dynasties, and political partisans chose this form in which to testify their loyalty to the reigning houses to which they owed allegiance.

The following are examples of the secular counterparts of the pious productions of Tesauro and his fellow Jesuits.

In 1654 a handsome folio was produced by the University of Vienna, entitled *Coronae Duodecim Caesarum*; it consists of twelve *elogia*, in a mixture of Latin, Greek, and Hebrew, in praise of twelve chosen Emperors belonging to the House of Habsburg (Plate 54).

[1] A specimen half-way between the pious and the political appeared in Vienna in 1683: *Rex Admirabilis, sive Vita S. Ladislai Regis Hungariae Historico-Politica*, by Stephanus Tarnoczi, S.J.; this contained fifty *elogia*, each of them at least 200 lines long. Tarnoczi was also the author of *Princeps Angelicus, sive Vita S. Emerici Ducis Hungariae*, Vienna, 1680, which consisted of twenty-eight lapidary *elogia*.

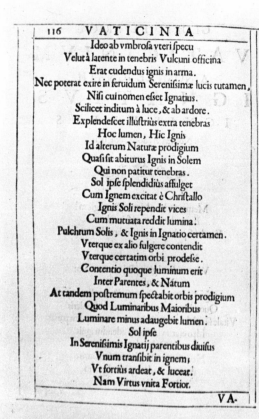

Ideo ab vmbrofa vteri fpecu
Velut à latente in tenebris Vulcuni officina
Erat cudendus ignis in arma.
Nec poterat exire in feruidum Serenifsimæ lucis tutamen,
Nifi cui nomen efset Ignatius.
Scilicet inditum à luce , & ab ardore.
Explendefcet illuftriùs extra tenebras
Hoc lumen , Hic Ignis
Id alterum Naturæ prodigium
Quafi fit abiturus Ignis in Solem
Qui non patitur tenebras.
Sol ipfe fplendidiùs affulget
Cum Ignem excitat è Chriftallo
Ignis Soli rependit vices
Cum mutuata reddit lumina.
Pulchrum Solis , & Ignis in Ignatio certamen.
Vterque ex alio fulgere contendit
Vterque certatim orbi prodefse.
Contentio quoque luminum erit
Inter Parentes , & Nátum
At tandem poftremum fpectabit orbis prodigium
Quod Luminaribus Maioribus
Luminare minus adaugebit lumen.
Sol ipfe
In Serenifsimis Ignatij parentibus diuifus
Vnum tranfibit in ignem;
Vt fortiùs ardeat , & luceat.
Nam Virtus vnita Fortior.

VA.

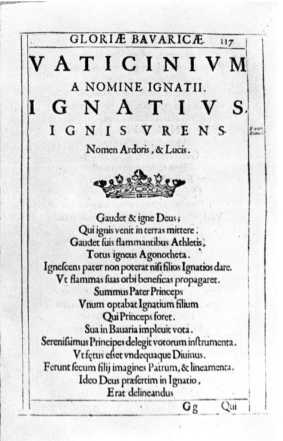

VATICINIVM
A NOMINE IGNATII.
IGNATIVS.
IGNIS VRENS
Nomen Ardoris , & Lucis.

Gaudet & igne Deus ;
Qui ignis venit in terras mittere :
Gaudet fuis flammantibus Athletis,
Totus igneus Agonotheta.
Ignefcens pater non poterat nifi filios Ignatios dare.
Vt flammas fuas orbi beneficas propagaret.
Summus Pater Princeps
Vnum optabat Ignatium filium
Qui Princeps foret.
Sua in Bauaria impleuit vota.
Serenifsimus Principes delegit votorum inftrumenta.
Vt fętus efset vndequaque Diuinus.
Ferunt fecum filij imagines Patrum , & lineamenta.
Ideo Deus præfertim in Ignatio ,
Erat delineandus

Gg   Qui

55. *Vaticinia Gloriae Bavaricae* (Venice, 1663), pp. 116–17.

Four years later, the same university produced another folio, *Imperium Romano-Germanicum*, containing fifty lapidary *elogia* by Nicolaus Avancinus, S.J., each of them about 200 lines long, in praise of the Emperors from Charlemagne to Leopold I.

Another book of this kind was published in Venice in 1663 by G.-M. Maraviglia, a Professor of the University of Padua, under the title *Vaticinia Gloriae Bavaricae* (Plate 55). The author takes every living member of the ruling House of Bavaria and contrives for each an 'augury' in lapidary Latin, inspired by the legends and symbols connected with his name.

In 1664, a splendid folio appeared in Nuremberg entitled *Mausoleum Regni Apostolici Regum et Ducum* (Plate 56). This consisted of lapidary *elogia*, in Latin and German, of the rulers of Hungary, Dukes and Kings, from the earliest times. A tragic historical interest attaches to this book, for its author, Count Francis de Nadasdi, was executed only a year or two after its publication for his part in a conspiracy against the ruling Emperor, Leopold.

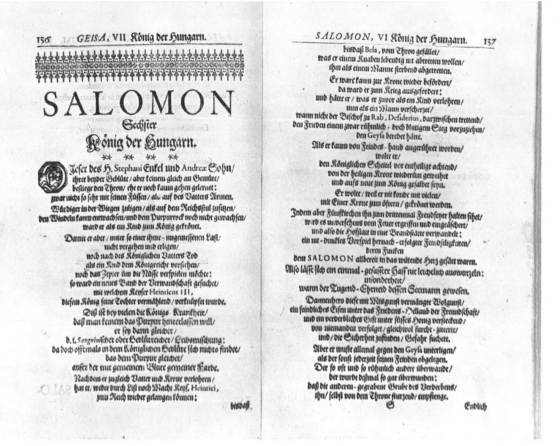

56. *Mausoleum Regum et Ducum* (Nuremberg, 1664), pp. 136-7.

It was not only for political panegyric that the form was employed: it was also made to serve the purposes of lampoon and satire: 'hoc seculo', says Weise, 'ab argutis laudibus' writers had proceeded 'ad argutiores Satyras', and he suggests that in this direction also it was the Jesuits that led the way, quoting a number of lapidary lampoons, published all over Europe, on the death of Wallenstein in 1634. These presumably were printed as broadsheets. An example from England is the broadsheet (panegyrical, not satirical) published on the death of General Monk in 1670.

A thicker crop, according to Weise, had grown up in Germany during the twenty years before he published his book in 1678: 'plena Satyrarum ac judiciorum de Magnatis publicorum Seges'. The pioneer in this field, he says, was the author of a pamphlet—*Collegium Electorale*—about the Electoral College, which came out without author's name or place of publication in 1658. This was one of the first of a series of anonymous pamphlets and booklets that appeared in Germany in the years 1657–77, some a mere half-dozen pages

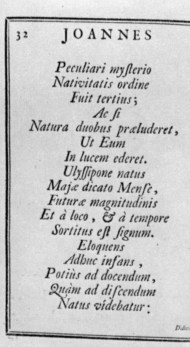

57. Johann Frischmann, *Causae Regum Belligerantium* (1657), pp. 128–9.

58. *Joannes Portugalliae Reges* (Lisbon, 1741), pp. 32–3.

long, others running to thirty, sixty, or nearly a hundred pages—all on the political problems of the day, all in Latin, and all in the same lapidary style. More than twenty of these have been shown to be the productions of Johann Frischmann, a Professor of Strasbourg University.[1]

Frischmann's *magnum opus* is a lapidary political history, tracing the causes of the recent and contemporary wars between Sweden and Poland and Burgundy and France. Plate 57 reproduces pp. 128–9 of this strange book— surely the most remarkable example of its kind: it is no less than 220 pages long.[2]

The most remarkable lapidary work in English that I have come across is Francis Quarles's *Memorials upon the Death of Sir Robert Quarles,* 1639, a little book consisting of an elegy of 253 lines upon the death of the poet's brother. In reprinting this work (in Quarles's *Complete Works,* Chertsey Worthies Library, III (1881), 27) Grosart obscures the fact that, though continuous, it consists of fourteen *elogia* of equal length (save that one, anomalously, is nineteen lines long), each of which occupies, in the original edition, a single page. So far as I know, this is the only *carmen lapidarium* on such a scale attempted by Quarles or any of his contemporaries in English.

EPILOGUE

I must content myself with the briefest of epilogues. The lapidary book died, so far as I have been able to discover, with the seventeenth century, though there are a few survivals; a splendid example occurs in Portugal as late as 1741 (Plate 58). Epigraphists thereafter confined themselves to stone or to the wood or canvas of the festal or funeral *apparatus*; their texts were apt to be lengthy, elaborate, and excessively 'lineated' without much regard to the meaning of the text, as in the typical English eighteenth-century epitaph; and though composers no longer tried to rival the Baroque wit of Tesauro and his contemporaries, their style remained florid and verbose.

Then, in the third quarter of the century, classicism reasserted itself: Stefano

---

[1] See *Johann Frischmann, ein Publizist des 17. Jahrhunderts,* by Paul Wentzcke, a doctoral thesis published at Strasbourg in 1904.

[2] I suspect it may be to Frischmann's publications that Weise is referring when he says (p. 290), in a passage concerning 'integri tractatus' composed in lapidary style, 'Ut taceam Scripta anonyma de Statu Europae passim publicata, quorum vel ideo mentionem prolixiorem nunc refugio, quia sine certo teste loqui nondum est animus.' I have appended (see p. 135) a list of publications in lapidary style attributed to Frischmann in Wentzcke's thesis.

Antonio Morcelli with his *De Stilo Inscriptionum* (1779) cleansed the Augean stables of epigraphy and inaugurated a new classical era of inscriptional writing. Concision of form, simplicity of idea, and purity of vocabulary became the rule, and the epigraphists of the day found their perfect typographer in Bodoni. An almost Grecian severity characterised the funeral displays of the period; they were splendid but austere; the catafalque erected in Milan Cathedral in 1802 for Mgr Filippo Visconti (Plate 59) strikingly illustrates the revolution in taste since Tesauro and Juglar designed *apparatus* for similar occasions a hundred and fifty years before. The epitaph or honorary inscription, after Morcelli, was more strictly classical both in style and in vocabulary; a typical example is the *Fastes* published by Didot in 1804 to celebrate the triumphs of Buonaparte (Plate 60). This book was something of a reversion to seventeenth-century precedent, for the inscriptions in it were composed simply for the press and were never inscribed on actual monuments.

Pierre-Sylvain Maréchal, a prolific miscellaneous writer, went further still along this backward path. He published in Paris in 1800 his *Histoire Universelle en Style Lapidaire*, a volume of nearly two hundred pages, rigidly lineated and printed in capital letters throughout (Plate 61). Its form and style may be inferred from its conclusion:

ENFANS DES HOMMES!

TELS ONT ÉTÉ VOS PÈRES,

MÉCHANS PAR LEUR IGNORANCE

MALHEUREUX PAR LEURS FAUTES:

PLAIGNEZ-LES

NE LES IMITEZ PAS.

59. Catafalque of Mgr Filippo Visconti, Archbishop of Milan (Milan, 1802).

(30)

VII.

TROIS JOURS DE SUITE
IL MET L'ENNEMI
EN DÉROUTE
AUX BORDS DE LA CHIESE
ET DU LAC DE GARDA
LES II, III, ET IV
AOUST.

(31)

VII.

HOSTIS
PER . TRIDVVM
FVSVS
AD . CLEVSIM . ET . BENACVM
IV . NON.
III . NON.
PRID . NON . SEXTIL.

60. Didot, *Fastes* (Paris, 1804), pp. 30–1.

CLXXXIV

LA HIRE ET XAINTRAILLES,
LA FAYETTE ET LA TRIMOUILLE,
MIEUX SERVI QU'UN BON MAITRE
PAR JACQUES CŒUR ET TANNEGUI DU CHATEL,
ET PAR LE PEUPLE
QUI REÇOIT LA TAILLE
SANS MURMURER.

UN ENNEMI DOMESTIQUE,
PIRE POUR CHARLES QUE LES ANGLAIS,
EMPOISONNE SES DERNIERS JOURS.
LE DAUPHIN
SE MONTROIT IMPATIENT
DE DEVENIR LOUIS XI.

UNE GRANDE CATASTROPHE
FAISOIT ALORS
TREMBLER L'EUROPE.
MAHOMET II
S'EMPARE DE CONSTANTINOPLE.

FUYANT DES VAINQUEURS
FIERS DE LEUR IGNORANCE,
LA GRÈCE-SAVANTE

CLXXXV

TROUVE UN ASYLE
AU VATICAN
PAR LES SOINS DE NICOLAS V.

EN FRANCE,
LE CHASTE BAISER DE LA DAUPHINE,
DONNÉ
AUX MUSES ET A L'ÉLOQUENCE
SUR LA BOUCHE D'ALAIN CHARTIER,
HATE
LA RENAISSANCE DES LETTRES.
ALORS AUSSI,
JEAN DE BRUGES
PEINT LE PREMIER A L'HUILE,
ET
FONDE L'ÉCOLE FLAMANDE.

MAIS
LES DEUX PLUS BEAUX MONUMENS
DE L'INTELLIGENCE HUMAINE,
ET QUI SEULS ÉGALENT
LES MODERNES AUX ANCIENS,
L'INVENTION DE L'IMPRIMERIE
ET
LA DÉCOUVERTE DU NOUVEAU-MONDE,

24

61. Sylvain Maréchal, *Histoire Universelle en Style Lapidaire* (Paris, 1800), pp. 184–5.

APPENDIX

Publications in 'lapidary' style attributed to Frischmann in Paul Wentzcke's thesis, *Johann Frischmann* (1904), see above, p. 131. The place of publication is given in the two instances where it is known.

Animorum in Europa, et vicina Asia motus De Suecici belli motu in Polonia. 64 pp. Gryphiswaldiae, 1656; 'recusi et aucti', 75 pp. Upsala, 1656.

Collegium Electorale de eligendo Romanorum Imperatore, 60 pp. 1657.

Collegium reliquorum Imperii Deputatorum ad Collegium Electorale, 43 pp. 1657. Editio auctior et correctior, 98 pp. 1658.

Moguntini labores Electorales, 45 pp. 1657.

Causae Regum heri et hodie inter se belligerantium, 220 pp. 1657.

Censura Censurae in Collegium Electorale amicae, 40 pp. 1658.

Labores Electorii sive Solennia Electionis et Consecrationis, 30 pp. 1658.

Responsio ad nuperam illam admonitionem, 32 pp. 1658.

Statera veritatem transgressa subversa, 20 pp. 1658.

Francisco Josepho Burrho Sacrum, 7 pp. 1660.

Acclamationes Anniversariae de pace orbi reddita, 46 pp. 1661.

Classicum belli Christiani, 37 pp. 1661.

Triumphus Honoris, 5 pp. 1662.

Pietas Francica, 41 pp. n.d.

Fallacis Fortunae et Mortalitatis vivum Exemplum, 6 pp. n.d.

Collegium Electorale de eligendo Romanorum Imperatore Addita Censura Censurae in illud Amicae, 60 pp. 1658.

Comitia Warsovica de eligendo Polonorum rege, 24 pp. 1669.

Batavia Triumphata, 15 pp. 1672.

Pax Vobis, 20 pp.

Concertata Pax Germaniae, 32 pp. } in *Diarium Europaeum,* 1677

Praevia seu adumbrata Theresiana pax Germaniae, 22 pp. } vol. XXXIV.

Pacis appendix Germaniae, 13 pp.

IV

CONCLUSION

I said at the beginning of this course of lectures that though the field they set out to cover was a narrow one, there were two topics in them that might be not without a wider interest: they concerned a remarkable and little-known extravagance of literary fashion, and they raised an intriguing aesthetic question about literary method.

In this last lecture I should like to offer a few reflections on that literary fashion and on that aesthetic question.

The fashion was a strange one. It expressed, and satisfied, a taste that spread over Europe in the seventeenth century, a taste for a kind of writing that was neither verse nor ordinary prose. Compositions in this *genre* were distinguished from prose by being divided into lines of varying lengths, and from verse by the fact that the length of each line was determined by its meaning and not by any metrical scheme. In the most extravagant examples, each line contained an epigram, or conceit, or 'point'. The form was derived from the lineated inscription, as developed in the sixteenth century from the classical originals that had so much excited the humanists of the early Renaissance.

What was it that made this kind of writing attractive to writers in the seventeenth century? The critics of the time suggested that their contemporaries had become tired of the restrictions imposed by metre and adopted this mode because it allowed them more licence in language and metaphor than prose, even oratorical prose, and more licence of form than verse; it did not confine them to prose diction, nor did it tie them down by metrical rules; the *Ars Lapidaria* lay mid-way, as they put it, between the *Ars Oratoria* and the *Ars Poetica*.

This, I suspect, is at best only half an explanation of what took place: no doubt the people who wrote in this manner relished the freedom of composition that it allowed them, but that does not explain why they looked for freedom along this line rather than another. No doubt they enjoyed its novelty, but that does not explain why they should have fallen for novelty of this particular kind. After all, if you chafed at the strictness of quantitative classical metres, you could write in the vernacular; Italian allowed greater freedom than Latin in the moulding of line and stanza; and even if you stuck to Latin, there were other directions in which you could experiment, whether in conformity to the rules of classical metre or in defiance of them. It was not long since Benedetto Lampridio, in Rome, had experimented with the Latin Pindaric, a hotch-potch in which lines of all kinds, exemplifying various metres, were jumbled together according to the taste and fancy of the composer. And it was just at this time that Mario Bettini of Bologna, under the pseudonym of Dionysius Ronsfertus, was trying to popularise in Italy and France a totally new and much freer form of Latin verse depending not upon quantity but upon accent.[1] Bettini was a Jesuit, and his system seems to have been widely adopted for the choruses of the plays acted in the Jesuit schools all over Catholic Europe. But neither Lampridio nor Bettini achieved such popular success as Emanuele Tesauro of Turin, with his quasi-inscriptional compositions, half-way between prose and verse.

This new style of writing grew naturally, I think, out of the conditions described in my third lecture; it was a result of the increasing popularity during the sixteenth century of the lineated inscription, displayed not only on public and private buildings and on sepulchral monuments but also on temporary structures manufactured for pageants and processions on festal or funereal occasions. The tablets, shields, and plaques with which these machines were adorned afforded a perfect opportunity for the display of that Baroque wit which just at this time was invading literature both in poetry and in prose. The attraction of a form in which every line must have the force of an epigram was irresistible to writers who were anxious above all things to display their wit, and such writers exploited to the full the ambiguity of the word *epi-gramma*, which had always been capable of meaning either an inscription or any piece of pointed writing.

Then came a second temptation: to spread one's self still further, and to do so on paper; the *carmen lapidarium*—line upon line, concept upon concept—was a perfect vehicle for the extravagant panegyric and the political lampoon. So there blossomed a new kind of broadsheet 'poetry'—the 'Poesis Politica' practised by Frischmann and described by Christian Weise.

[1] See my paper 'Sarbiewski's *Silviludia* and their Italian source', *Oxford Slavonic Papers*, VIII (1958), 1–48.

137

It was but a short step from publishing lapidary broadsheets to manufacturing whole books in this fashion, by linking one *elogium* to another and making biography or history out of a series of *lemmata* each treated in lapidary style. Plates 52 and 54–7 display some of the fruits of this curious fashion.

The fashion did not outlast the century it was born in. Burckhardt condenses the whole matter into a characteristically pregnant phrase: 'the epigraph', he says, 'continued to flourish till the seventeenth century, when it perished finally of bombast'. Burckhardt was speaking of the Baroque inscription upon stone; the lapidary book, the epigraph extended in print, flourished likewise, and was as surely, or even more surely, doomed to extinction. The form was designed for public display; it was meant for him who runs to read; its aim was to catch the eye and to take the intelligence by surprise; if it is extended unduly it teases and tires both sight and brain; and the matter—an epigram in every line—is, as the composers were themselves uneasily aware, stuff of which only snacks or *bonnes bouches* can be made; you must take only a little at a time; you cannot depend on it for nourishment.

The demand for such books really died with the seventeenth century, though it lingered on here and there in Europe well into the eighteenth; the elaborate specimen from Portugal belonging to the 1740s shown in Plate 58 is, it seems, the last product of the taste for whole books printed in this style. It is true that, as we have seen, an *Histoire Universelle en Style Lapidaire* was published in Paris in 1800 (Plate 61), but I should class this as a resurrection rather than a survival of the *genre*.

The *Histoire Universelle* was an exception to the general rule, in that it was not in Latin but in French, and this prompts the question why this style of writing should not have flourished in the vernacular languages of Europe. The answer is twofold. The witty writers, the lapidary panegyrists and pamphleteers, wanted as wide a public as they could get for their productions, and if you had that aim in view, Latin, even in the late seventeenth century, was the only language. Arithmaeus, when he reproduced Camden's Westminster Abbey guide-book at Frankfurt in 1617, omitted the English translations of the Latin epitaphs: 'Anglicam enim linguam paucissimi intelligunt'; Frischmann would have limited the international audience he sought for his pamphlets about Imperial elections, had he written them in German; in Italy there was hardly yet established a *volgare* as generally accepted and intelligible as was Latin throughout the peninsula. Furthermore, as we have seen, the style was exploited principally by the Jesuits, who naturally used the language of the universal Church.

There was another consideration favouring Latin, one that applied not only to broadsheets and books intended for an international audience but to every epigraph or inscription: Latin is the ideal language for lapidary composition. It is ideal for that purpose because it is both concise and flexible. Conciseness is essential where the length of the line (and this means usually the shortness of the line) is a main preoccupation of the writer; flexibility helps to the same end.

Latin is a concise language, partly because it is inflected and can therefore do without 'to' and 'of' and other troublesome little words; partly because it has no definite or indefinite article and none of the particles that are, for an epigraphist, the bane of the Greek language. Latin is flexible because of the wide scope it allows in the use of participial phrases and its great freedom of word-order. This makes it easier to arrange what you have to say in appropriate lines: you can transpose the verbal pieces in your mosaic, in order to fit them together effectively, with much greater freedom than is possible in German, for instance, or in English.

Was this episode in the history of literature (and of book-production), after all, of any importance? Is it worth even a passing glance from the historian? That depends, perhaps, on what is intended by the word 'important'.

Shortly before I undertook the composition of this course of lectures, I explained what they were to be about to an ex-Professor of History in the University of Cambridge. I introduced him to Emanuele Tesauro and showed him some of the strange products of that writer's wit. I described how the lapidary kind of writing was spread by the Society of Jesus into the remotest corners of Europe, and how pamphlets in lapidary form were used as a weapon by political polemicists. My friend was interested and even enthusiastic; he said that I had hit upon an excellent subject, a subject very suitable for the Sandars Lectures. 'But of course', he added, with a slight change of expression, 'it is (isn't it?) what G. M. Trevelyan used to call "fundamentally piffle"?'

This observation implied, I think, no disrespect for the Sandars Lecturer or for his audiences. It did not even imply any grave disrespect for Tesauro. The

Professor simply meant that this effort to create a new literary *genre* got nowhere; it did not awake or employ the genius of any great, or even considerable, writer; it had no lasting effect at all. Tesauro and his imitators were ploughing the sand; they proved the barrenness of that particular tract of literary ground.

That is true. But we should hesitate, I think, before we write off such literary experimenters with contempt. Single-minded, whole-hearted devotion to an artistic theory, however absurd, is not necessarily a thing to be despised; the more absurd the theory, the more touching and in a way perhaps the more admirable the devotion; the martyr in a lost cause is still a martyr.

Before we dismiss the composers of palindromes and acrostichal and serpentine verses, of figured poetry and visual puns, of interminable *elogia*, of lapidary biographies, of whole histories written in the form of book-long epitaphs, let us remember others nearer our own day who have devoted their gifts to efforts equally bizarre and equally unfruitful, and whose endeavours are regarded with awed solemnity by critics who would no doubt dismiss the lapidary *genre* as mere trifling.

'Figured' verses were a favourite device of Guillaume Apollinaire, who often amused himself by composing 'Calligrammes', which represented by their shapes the things that they described—a downpour of rain, a man smoking a pipe, a bursting bomb—and often, also, arranged his lines in odd and meaningless configurations on the page, with no other apparent intention than to startle the reader, to compel his attention, and to make him study the text with freshly awakened eyes (Plate 62).

Two of the most admired and most sophisticated literary artists of modern times, Stéphane Mallarmé and Ezra Pound, have played games with words as grotesque as anything attempted by Tesauro and his followers. Many passages in Pound's *Cantos* depend for their effect upon typographical devices to which it is impossible to do justice simply by reading out the text. But the supreme instance of a piece of literature that depends for its effect upon its visual layout is Mallarmé's *Un Coup de Dés jamais n'abolira le Hasard* (Plate 63).

Like Tesauro, Mallarmé pushed to the point of absurdity a theory about literary presentation. But there was a difference between Mallarmé and Tesauro: Mallarmé was both a genius and a poet, and Tesauro, I am afraid, was neither. This means, unfortunately, that the time spent by Mallarmé in riding

CALLIGRAMMES

Écoute s'il pleut écoute s'il pleut

puis	sol	des	con	la
é	dats	Flan	fon	pluie
cou	a	dres	dez-	si
tez	veu	à	vous	ten
tom	gles	l'	a	dre
ber	per	a	vec	la
la	dus	go	l'	pluie
pluie	par	nie	ho	si
si	mi	sous	ri	dou
ten	les	la	zon	ce
dre	che	pluie	beaux	
et	vaux	fi	ê	
si	de	ne	tres	
dou	fri	la	in	
ce	se	pluie	vi	
	sous	si	si	
	la	ten	bles	
	lu	dre	sous	
	ne	et	la	
	li	si	pluie	
	qui	dou	fi	
	de	ce	ne	

62. Guillaume Apollinaire, part of a page from *Calligrammes*.

his hobby-horse through the desert was even worse wasted than the time spent in the same way by Tesauro: Mallarmé might have put it to so much better a use.

And yet behind both Tesauro's and Mallarmé's experiments there lies an idea: in each case it is the same idea, and it is an idea not without interest and not altogether without value. Both of them thought that a writer, by addressing himself to the eye as well as to the intellect, might refine and reinforce the appeal of his work. I dealt in my second lecture with the hybrid compositions that painters and sculptors have produced by incorporating written texts into works of art whose main (and natural) constituents are visual images, or non-figurative arrangements of line and colour and form. What Mallarmé and Tesauro, each in his own way, were both trying to do was to produce a hybrid composition that is something like the converse of this—a literary work of which visual form should be an essential constituent.

Mallarmé tried to do this by managing the effect of his word-symbols as they impinged upon the mind of his readers, varying the size (and so the clarity and vividness) of the symbols themselves and their relations in space—that is, upon the page. Tesauro and his followers relied only upon variations in

C'ÉTAIT
issu stellaire

CE SERAIT
pire
non
davantage ni moins
indifféremment mais autant

63. Stéphane Mallarmé,
pages from *Un Coup de Dés*.

the length of the lines their pieces were composed of. If Mallarmé's failure
was the more conspicuous, that is because he attempted so much more than
the lapidary writers; his complicated and sophisticated efforts overtaxed even
more heavily than theirs the visual potentialities of the printed word.

Tesauro's more modest failure was due in the first place to the fact that he
went on far too long. Extended passages of lapidary writing bore us in the same
way that long passages of free verse can bore us; there is no formal pattern,
as there is in metrical verse, to beguile us with the double pleasure of recog-
nising first conformity to the norm and then divagation from it. When
Tesauro attempts to distract his readers and hold their attention by a succession
of conceits, he only wearies them the more.

Yet the instrument with which both Mallarmé and the lapidary writers were

LE NOMBRE

EXISTÂT-IL
autrement qu'hallucination éparse d'agonie

COMMENÇÂT-IL ET CESSÂT-IL
sourdant que nié et clos quand apparu
enfin
par quelque profusion répandue en rareté
SE CHIFFRÂT-IL

évidence de la somme pour peu qu'une
ILLUMINÂT-IL

LE HASARD

Choit
la plume
rythmique suspens du sinistre
s'ensevelir
aux écumes originelles
naguères d'où sursauta son délire jusqu'à une cime
flétrie
par la neutralité identique du gouffre

in their differing ways experimenting is one that is capable of producing, within a limited range, subtle and even moving effects. For they were right in thinking that a reader may be affected in the very act of appreciating the meaning of a sequence of words by the visual form in which they are presented to him: the quality of the impact that a piece of writing makes upon our minds may be in part determined by the layout, and particularly by the lineation, of the text in which it is embodied upon the page.

We may perceive the truth of this if we try to imagine how different our conception of 'poetry' would be if all the poetry we had ever read had been printed like prose. How different also must be the meaning of the word 'poetry' to someone who is accustomed to seeing poetry in print from the meaning it bears to someone who has been blind from birth! Similarly, the impression we carry in our minds of the text of the Bible, or of any passage from it—say, the Sermon on the Mount—is determined to a large extent by the fact that we have always seen it printed in 'verses'.[1]

This is true also of particular poems and other passages of writing. Take Pater's famous description of Leonardo's Mona Lisa, chosen by W. B. Yeats to stand first in his anthology of modern verse. Yeats evidently did not think that the poetic quality of this passage was a sufficient justification for including it in a verse anthology as it stood; so he printed it as free verse, in lines of varying length. What made Yeats re-shape the passage exactly as he did? Was it the rhythm of the lines into which he divided it? Or the need for pauses that could not be sufficiently indicated by punctuation marks? One cannot say. What at least is clear is that it is necessary, in Yeats's view, to *see* the passage so printed if one is to appreciate it properly. Yet we may ask: does it really become verse, does it cease to be prose, as a result of his re-shaping?

This raises the question of 'free' verse: what is it that determines the length of its component lines? And why, if it comes to that, should all the lines of a prose passage (except the line that concludes a paragraph) be of equal length? Why is it not our practice to print prose so that each line is of the length that the author considers most effective? Is the reason simply, as a historical survey seems to suggest, an economic one: print derives from manuscript; and manuscript from stone; stone-cutters and scribes wished to waste as little as possible of their precious material, and so prolonged every line to the edge of the surface upon which they worked?

Whether or not it was owing to such material considerations that prose came to be printed as it is, we nowadays accept it as a natural law that it should be printed so. It is salutary that such laws should be challenged from time to time, as this law was challenged in the seventeenth century by the lapidary book-makers and as the conventional laws of verse were challenged by Mallarmé two hundred years later. The results, however, vindicated the practice that they refused to follow: the literary effect that can be achieved by visual presentation is limited, and their efforts to go beyond its limits were a failure. None the less, within those limits lies a narrow yet not negligible margin, and that margin is the field of the epigraphic art.

[1] Messrs Heinemann some years ago sponsored an edition of the Bible in which the division into verses was eliminated; it was called, significantly, 'The Bible intended to be read as Literature'.

INDEX